D0667912

A Living Savior

Devotions for pALS (people with ALS)

And their caregivers and families

Sharon Colwell

A Living Savior:
Devotions for pALS (people with ALS)
And Their Caregivers and Families

© Sharon Colwell, 2022
All rights reserved
Published by Kindle Direct Publishing

Cover Art: "The Living Water" watercolor painting © Sharon Colwell

All Scripture quotations, unless otherwise indicated, are taken from the Holy Bible, New International Version®, NIV®. Copyright ©1973, 1978, 1984, 2011 by Biblica, Inc.™ Used by permission of Zondervan. All rights reserved worldwide. www.zondervan.com The "NIV" and "New International Version" are trademarks registered in the United States Patent and Trademark Office by Biblica, Inc.™

Scripture quotations marked (NLT) are taken from the Holy Bible, New Living Translation, copyright ©1996, 2004, 2015 by Tyndale House Foundation. Used by permission of Tyndale House Publishers, Carol Stream, Illinois 60188. All rights reserved.

Scripture quotations marked (NKJV) are taken from the New King James Version (NKJV). Scripture taken from the New King James Version®. Copyright © 1982 by Thomas Nelson. Used by permission. All rights reserved.

Library of Congress

ISBN: 9798432146168
Imprint: Independently published
Nonfiction > Religion > Biblical Meditations > New Testament
Nonfiction > Religion > Devotional

Kindle Direct Publishing

Book and eBook available at Amazon.com

Sharon Colwell takes us on her personal journey with ALS. She writes with empathy as a fellow person with ALS and giving a glimpse into the heartache and suffering of people with ALS. She guides the one suffering and the caregiver to look to a Living Savior through the Scriptures and the names of Jesus that bring comfort, help and hope. And interspersed through the devotional are prayers to wash over your soul and cleanse and encourage your heart. A devotional worth reading and rereading.

- *Dr. Michael Boyle, Retired Professor, Moody Bible Institute, Author, and Interim Pastor*

~~~

I am so moved as I read these messages of loss, and then hearing Sharon's experience of allowing God to use the suffering and replace the loss as only He can. Then to take those miraculous revelations and selflessly offer them to others suffering similar losses. Absolutely wonderful and remarkable. These messages of encouragement are the epitome of 2 Corinthians 1:3-4, comforting others with the comfort she has found as she looks to a Living Savior. I believe this is one of the principal purposes of the body of Christ as we travel a variety of challenging journeys this side of heaven. I think of Paul, the writer of much of the New Testament, as he struggles with his losses, writing to the churches from a prison cell that he will never leave on this earth, and still encouraging many people he doesn't know and will never have the opportunity to meet. He even says things like, "now I rejoice in what I am suffering for you." (Colossians 1:24 NIV) This is the same spirit I sense as I read what Sharon has written, the Spirit helping her, and then helping especially those of you reading these words.

I share several things with Sharon...my son and her daughter building a life together, co-grandparents of five grandchildren, a birthdate, many years of friendship, and even some suffering in recent years. I have had the opportunity to see her live and respond with grace in the good and the tough times. These challenges with ALS take the difficult times to another level that I do not know and yet I have grown and been challenged by reading what Sharon has experienced and then shared with us. My prayer is that those of you fighting the fight with ALS will allow God's Spirit and these words to be a "very present help in time of trouble." (Psalm 46:1b NKJV)

Thank you, Sharon, for allowing God to so sweetly use you. I am thankful to God for you and I am very proud of you and your efforts in writing these comforting and powerful insights.

I share one other all important thing with Sharon...a Living Savior!

"My flesh and my heart may fail, but God is the strength of my heart and my portion forever." (Psalm 73:26 NIV)

- *Mike Gates, Friend, Fellow Grandparent and Pastor of Living Hope Church, Elk Grove Village, Illinois*

~~~

In 1984 my Dad was diagnosed with ALS. Doctors gave him no hope and sent him home with "less than two years to live." But they underestimated the incredible love he would receive from friends and family, especially from my mother. He lived almost seven years, and though his body was steadily failing him, he grew closer to God, deeper in his faith, and had a Peace that was beyond our understanding.

Visitors, however, did not do as well. They felt awkward and struggled for the right words to say, never realizing that what he needed most was simply for them to be there. In time many —even some close friends and family—stopped visiting. They wanted to encourage him but did not know what to do. So in 1997 I started a ministry to teach them how.

Over the years I've searched for new ways to encourage one another—seminars, conferences, speaking engagements, books, our weekly A Note of Encouragement—but never thought about a devotional. That is, until Sharon sent me a copy of "A Living Savior" to review. And then it was all I could think about.

This devotional is an incredible work by an incredible lady. Imagine being in the grips of something so hopeless, yet using that very experience to share hope...<u>real</u> hope...with others going through the same struggle. Not many would consider doing such a thing, even less actually trying. But Sharon did, and she has!

Throughout "A Living Savior" Sharon shares what has happened in her life. Then she speaks of her deep love for Jesus who is by her side every step of the way...drawing ever closer to her day by day, strengthening her faith, and giving her that Peace my Dad knew so long ago. And she shares how He is doing the same for each of us...right now...regardless of our circumstances, good or bad. Through wisdom, humor, and love, she leads us to what matters most—following a Living Savior.

- *Chuck Graham, Founder and Executive Director of Ciloa International Ministries (<u>www.Ciloa.org</u>), Speaker, Author, and not a half bad encourager*

~~~

Many who are diagnosed with ALS are told by doctors to go home and get your affairs in order before you die. As a follower of Jesus Christ, Sharon Colwell has found greater purpose and meaning in each day. She wrote "A Living Savior" to share how God is meeting her in every loss along the Bulbar ALS journey and to encourage all affected by ALS with Scriptures that provide strength and courage. "A Living Savior" is a great reminder that we can really live an abundant life of Christ, even with ALS.

- *Ann Chastain, Co-founder of the "Blessing Love Box" group, and member of the Ciloa International Ministries Board of Directors*

~~~

We are all stewards of the pain God allows in our lives. Sharon Colwell has stewarded that pain well and put words of hope and healing onto the page.

I believe this book is going to be a great comfort to those who are walking through a diagnosis or walking with someone they love.

- *Chris Fabry, host of "Chris Fabry Live: Back Fence" on Moody radio, and Author*

~~~

In this Biblically-based devotional, "A Living Savior", Sharon communicates openly and honestly about her own personal struggle with ALS. Sharon could have sat in her grief and pain, counting what she has lost. But instead, she has turned to Jesus who has shown Himself to be her mighty counselor and comforter, her strength and help! Sharon shares Scripture with us that God has used to change her thoughts and her perspective as she faces this hardship. She offers thought-provoking questions that lead each of us to examine our own hearts and lives—whether or not we are personally suffering from ALS or know someone facing this debilitating disease. My cousin had ALS and I wish there had been a devotional like this, at that time, that I could have given to him!

- *Cathy Kato, Missionary, ReachGlobal*

~~~

As a fellow traveler on this Bulbar ALS road, I applaud Sharon for looking to Christ for her strength. ALS can be a very lonely disease. Other people around us can't understand what we are feeling not being able to speak. Often they will ask a question and leave before I can type an answer. So much of the time I will type something to be part of the conversation, but the conversation has moved on. And then there is the continuing loss of function.

What can we do but look up? Look up to where true peace comes from. To God who is our strength. Sharon says it all so well, from her heartfelt prayers to the Scriptures she has chosen to complement her stories. Without God, how can people fight this disease?

- *Kay Timmons Parker, Co-founder of the "Blessing Love Box" group and fellow pALS*

~~~

As one of the pastors at Wheaton Bible Church, I have had the privilege of knowing Sharon and Tom Colwell for several years including five years before Sharon was diagnosed with ALS. Their strong engagement in God's kingdom is a blessing to many in our body. When Sharon was diagnosed with ALS, it was heartbreaking for all that know her. I knew Sharon's deep faith was going to be tested, but I sensed that the depth of Sharon's walk and her focus on Jesus would be her guide in this dark valley. "A Living Savior" is a testimony to just that. From the introduction through seven steps of loss upon loss, by God's grace, Sharon shows how God has not allowed this disease to take her focus off Him. From her loss of speech to loss of breathing, she allows her Living Savior to redirect her gaze beyond her loss to intently seeing Jesus as sufficient for her every need. May God allow Sharon's story to minister to pALS, to those that support them and help each reader follow the Jesus that has sustained Sharon.

- *Mark Irvin, Pastor of Community Life, Wheaton Bible Church, West Chicago, Illinois*

~~~

As someone who is also affected with this dreadful disease of ALS, I so appreciate the devotions included in this book, "A Living Savior", by Sharon Colwell.

As ALS progresses, it becomes more and more important that we are surrounded by people who can love and support us. However, this is not a reality for many of us. And, even if we do receive love and support from others, there is nothing like the love and support that Jesus Christ can provide and, of course, the hope for all of eternity for those of us who have placed our faith in Jesus—as our Lord and Savior.

This devotional, "A Living Savior", is such an encouragement and emphasizes that, through Jesus, we do have hope for eternity. As it says in God's Word, "May the God of hope fill you with all joy and peace as you trust in Him, so that you may overflow with hope by the power of the Holy Spirit." (Romans 15:13 NIV) This devotional provides encouragement to all of us. As we read it, I believe all of us will draw closer to Jesus. And, the devotional should help all of us get to know God's Word better, bask in it and trust God in that He will always be with us—especially during these challenging times.

I hope that all readers will meditate and get to know God's Word more fully each and every day. And, like me, I know Sharon hopes that everyone comes to a saving faith in Christ so that we can enjoy one another's company in Heaven—for all of eternity.

- *Steven J. Cochlan, Founder of the ALS Family of Faith and Board Member of Fellowship of Christian Athletes (Wrestling)*

~~~

I had not known anyone with ALS until Sharon shared her diagnosis one morning in our Sunday school class. Before that day, we had been praying for her, unsure of what the ailment was that she was suffering from. I'll never forget her face, and that of her husband, as they shared the news that it was ALS. We didn't even know what the prognosis would be. But God's light shone through both of them as they shared that morning, reassuring our class that our Most High God was in control.

Now over the year and months of seeing Sharon battle this disease, I have been struck by the Lord's beauty and grace

that shine through her. She truly radiates joy. "A Living Savior"
is such an encouragement to read and brings one closer to our
Lord. Hearts will be fortified as they are led through the seven
losses but find strength from God's Word. Readers will find
knowing Jesus in new and beautiful ways: as the Word, the
Bread of Life, the Giver of Living Water, our Vine, the Giver of
the Fruit of the Spirit, our Good Shepherd, and the Giver of the
Breath of Life. Sharon weaves stories from the Word of God,
helping you feel as if you were there, listening to Jesus speak
with comfort and care—The Living Savior

- *Andrew J. Schmutzer, PhD, Professor of Bible, Moody Bible Institute*

Prologue

For those of us with ALS (Amyotrophic Lateral Sclerosis, or Lou Gehrig's disease), day-by-day loss of function is so unpredictable and distressing. My diagnosis in the fall of 2020 left me determined to manage my symptoms well. I did research and fought against my losses, yet I would often castigate myself for my growing inabilities. I was rapidly losing my speech, and most often, I was losing my self-control.

What I now understand as "PBA" (Pseudobulbar Affect) was ruining my days with crying, anger, and inappropriate laughter. I was scaring myself as well as those around me with my lack of emotional control. I began seeking a counselor who could help me deal with these new problems. Christmas was approaching, and I didn't want to be out of control. However, I could find no counselors who were ready to take on an ALS patient.

My doctor recommended that I take a special medication just for PBA, and it helped my self-control greatly. Still, my prognosis was troubling. I wished I could talk to a counselor. It was then that the Lord reminded me of Isaiah 9:6.

> For to us a child is born,
> to us a son is given,
> and the government will be on his shoulders.
> And he will be called
> Wonderful Counselor, Mighty God,
> Everlasting Father, Prince of Peace.

Here was the answer! Jesus is my Wonderful Counselor. I would look to Him for help.

One day, while I was praying about my physical needs, the Lord brought to mind a new meaning for the ALS acronym, *Sharon, why not think instead of your need for "A Living Savior"?*

I began journaling my needs for Jesus as each function was lost. My speech was the first function to totally disappear. So, when I didn't have any words of my own, I looked to Jesus, my Wonderful Counselor, for help. Jesus reminded me that He is also the "Word". I delved even deeper into my study of the Word of God, the Bible, seeking to know Jesus better. Next, I lost my ability to eat, and Jesus reminded me that He is the "Bread of Life". Jesus would sustain me as I trusted in Him.

In every new loss of mine I found that Jesus already had a special way to bring me comfort. His familiar names in the Bible spoke to me in new ways. When I would feel anguished, Jesus would remind me that He had saved my heart from desperation. He could fill my heart with grace and joy instead. I began to delight in journaling how Jesus is such "A Living Savior" to me, especially as I now have ALS.

I hope this devotional, based on my thoughts and experiences of the last year, will bring you comfort as well. As we all undergo new losses, may the names of Jesus bring us all peace until we all meet our loving, living Savior face-to-face.

Sharon

Dedication

With grateful love to Christy, our wonderful daughter. She not only accompanies me on all my doctor visits, she also gently accompanies me emotionally and spiritually through the quagmire of this disease. Being with Christy is always a time I look forward to. Her faith in Christ and love of God (and me) bring joy and blessings to all who know her. And, our whole family rejoices in the words she started using as an 8-year-old: "I love you...Almost As Much As Jesus!" (AAMAJ!)

She is clothed with strength and dignity,
and she laughs without fear of the future.
26When she speaks, her words are wise,
and she gives instructions with kindness.

(Proverbs 31:25-26 NLT)

Contents

Praise be to the God and Father of our Lord Jesus Christ, the Father of compassion and the God of all comfort, ⁴who comforts us in all our troubles, so that we can comfort those in any trouble with the comfort we ourselves receive from God.

(2 Corinthians 1:3-4)

1. Loss of Speech – Jesus is the Word

Study the Word, that your faith may not stand in the wisdom of man, but in the power of God...A Bible that's falling apart usually belongs to someone who isn't!—Charles H. Spurgeon [1]

Loss of Speech

Loss of speech was my first indication that something was wrong. I had a sharp pain in my left ear and neck. Then I gradually became aware of slightly slurred speech. I could no longer say words with "L" and "K" sounds. In May 2020, I tried to say my grandson was "athletically inclined" but it was nearly impossible. In September, I was diagnosed with ALS, Amyotrophic Lateral Sclerosis. By Christmas, I'd totally lost my speech.

I had been a follower of Christ for many years. Church groups prayed for my healing, and friends sent gifts and arranged love-filled gatherings. But this was a new challenge.

If you are also part of a group of pALS (people with ALS) who have lost your speech, I sympathize with you. It's so heartbreaking to lose the ability to speak. I miss talking to my husband, my daughters, and to my grandkids in something other than a grunting "Chewbacca" voice. I miss all those spontaneous conversations with friends. I miss teaching. I miss leading a small group. I have a helpful speech app, but I found out sadly, that it has absolutely no personality to its voice. And, even if it did, it would not have been mine.

One day I cried out my frustrations to the Lord, slamming my hand on the table and groaning inside, "I can't even say a word anymore!" Then I felt the Lord's reply in my heart, "I am the Word." God seemed to be using this horrible disease of ALS to let me know I could rely more on His Word. I realized that even if I didn't have my own words anymore, I have Jesus in my life. I can speak in my heart to Him. And, I can hear Him speak to me through His Word.

We pALS used to be able to speak tens of thousands of words a day. But the Bible is filled with even thousands more words that are helpful to us. Are you finding yourself at a loss for words? Do you want God to speak to you? I remembered the song "Word of God Speak" written in 2002, by a favorite band of mine, MercyMe. The words spoke to my heart as they may speak to you, my pALS.

Prayer

Heavenly Father, let me start my prayer by echoing the lyrics of the song, "Word of God Speak." [2] The words of this song have taken on new meaning for me now that I have ALS. You know I cannot speak, but I want to hear You speak to me—Amen.

Word of God Speak

I'm finding myself at a loss for words
And the funny thing is it's okay.
The last thing I need is to be heard
But to hear what You would say.

Word of God speak!
Would You pour down like rain
Washing my eyes to see
Your majesty?

To be still and know
That You're in this place?
Please let me stay and rest
In Your holiness.
Word of God speak!

I'm finding myself in the midst of You
Beyond the music, beyond the noise.
All that I need is to be with You
And in the quiet hear Your voice.
Word of God speak!

Heavenly Father, I am truly "finding myself at a loss for words" as I am unable to speak. I need to let go of my frustration at my loss of speech, and to rest in Your holiness, knowing You have a good plan for my life.

When I'm immersed in Your Word, I can truly see more of Your majesty. I can actually find myself in Your presence. Beyond all the dissonance of my life, I can be with You, Lord God, and quietly hear You speak. Please speak to me today through Your Word and comfort me with Your voice —Amen.

Jesus is the Word

The opening of John's Gospel tells us:

> In the beginning was the Word, and the Word was with God, and the Word was God. [2]He was with God in the beginning. [3]Through him all things were made; without him nothing was made that has been made... [14]The Word became flesh and made his dwelling among us. (John 1:1-4,14)

"The Word became flesh!" The Word of God came alive in the incarnate Jesus. That's the Christmas story. The child born in Bethlehem was actually the Word of God in the flesh. God's Word, so praised by Old Testament writers, had come alive in Jesus, the embodiment of God's Word. The words that Jesus would later speak would astonish people because Jesus' words were the words of God.

But Luke's Gospel tells us more about Christ's birth, as the angels proclaimed:

> Today in the town of David a Savior has been born to you; he is the Messiah, the Lord. (Luke 2:11)

This tender little baby was not only the Word of God come alive. He was the Savior, Messiah and Lord! If I were alive at the time of Jesus, I would have wanted to hear His sermons as Messiah. But would I have followed every word He said? I would have longed to see His miracles as the Savior. I would have become astonished at His compassion. But would I have been healed? I might have witnessed His death, but would I have believed His resurrection as Lord? He would have called me to Himself, but how would I have responded?

Later, the apostle Paul would write about our response to Jesus.

> The **word** is near you; it is in your mouth and in your heart, that is, the message concerning faith that we proclaim: 9If you declare with your mouth, "Jesus is Lord," and believe in your heart that God raised him from the dead, you will be saved. 10For it is with your heart that you believe and are justified, and it is with your mouth that you profess your faith and are saved. 11As Scripture says, "Anyone who believes in him will never be put to shame." 12For there is no difference between Jew and Gentile—the same Lord is Lord

of all and richly blesses all who call on him, [13]for, "Everyone who calls on the name of the Lord will be saved." (Romans 10:8b-13, emphasis added)

God is calling all of us to believe in the gift of his Son Jesus, whom He sent as the Messiah and Savior of humanity. If we believe in our hearts and gratefully proclaim our faith, saying "Jesus is Lord," our everlasting Father God will welcome us to His family…now and for all eternity.

pALS Application

The Word of God came alive in Jesus—so now, when we read His words, He can come alive in our hearts. When we read His words, we hear Him talk with us each day. When we pray, we have a real conversation with Him. When we rest in His company as Emmanuel, which means "God with us," we are enjoying a real relationship with Him. Jesus, the Word of God, will assure us of His love for eternity. And that gives me hope and peace.

I like to substitute "Jesus" for the phrase "Your Word" in order to give me hope and peace. Here are a few examples from Scripture:

- Jesus (Your word) is a lamp for my feet, a light on my path. (Psalm 119:105)

Only the Lord knows what comes next on our journeys as pALS. We want to be held by His hand, for only He can show us His way.

- You are my refuge and my shield; I have put my hope in Jesus (Your word). (Psalm 119:114)

Certainly, we all need a refuge, a place to hide and be comforted. That place of refuge is in His Word, the comforting arms of our Savior, Jesus.

Many Old Testament Scriptures speak of the wonders of God's Word. Psalm 19 speaks specifically of His law, testimony, and judgments.

- They (the words of God) are more precious than gold, than much pure gold; they are sweeter than honey, than honey from the honeycomb. (Psalm 19:10)

If Jesus is truly the Word of God (and He is!) then knowing Him is precious and sweet.

These verses also showed me a special application for those of us pALS who can no longer speak. God reminded me that we can use our written words and actions to show our trust in Him. Our faith can shine through our disease, causing others to rejoice as they see our hope in the Word, Jesus. Psalm 119:74 says:

- May those who fear you rejoice when they see me, for I have put my hope in Jesus (your word).

Although my appearance may have changed (weight loss, drooling, withered skin, shortness of breath, an off-balance gait, etc.), people will actually "rejoice when they see me." Why is that? They will see that only Jesus can and does give me a rich hope.

Closing Prayer

Lord Jesus, I wish I'd had an opportunity to meet You in person 2,000 years ago. I would love to have heard Your words, seen Your face, touched Your hand, perhaps even to have been healed by You, and to know You are truly Emmanuel, God with us.

As I read the Word of God today, I trust You, Jesus, as my Savior and Lord. I bring my needs to You. Word of God, please come alive to me in a new way as I read the pages of

Scripture. While I cannot talk, please speak to me. Please show me more about Yourself, my Savior and the rescuer from all my sin and suffering. Help me know You better, as I have a conversation with You in my heart—Amen.

Reflections on Jesus as the Word

1. Do you want to hear God speak to you through His Word? Will you spend more time in His Word?

2. Do you have a favorite verse from God's Word? Write it here. Why is it your favorite verse? How does that verse reveal to you more of God's majesty or give you more hope?

3. Do you remember when you first welcomed Jesus into your life as "A Living Savior" to you? When was that? If you have not yet received His gift of love and forgiveness and promise of eternal life, will you do so now?

4. Our lives are not under our own control anyway. Will you surrender control to our loving Father God?

2. Loss of Ability to Eat – Jesus is the Bread of Life

When you are hungry for God, He will fill you. —*Jentezen Franklin* [3]

Bread of Life? Jesus lived up to the title. But an unopened loaf does a person no good. Have you received the bread? Have you received God's forgiveness? —*Max Lucado* [4]

The Loss of Eating Ability

It was so sad to lose my ability to speak. Yet I could use my speech app. And most of all, I could always have a conversation with God. But losing my ability to eat by mouth was even more devastating a loss. It brought along a constant drooling and the embarrassing inability to keep my lips closed. That meant I could no longer even pucker up for a "sloppy kiss", as my husband called it. More frightening were the frequent choking and swallowing spasms that my throat would make, even when I'd try to swallow something simple like applesauce or puree.

The loss of eating ability was a strangely emotional loss, too. I'd always been a "social diner," with a family that would often spend two hours around the dinner table. We'd pray together before we ate, enjoy food that each of us had brought, and promise to exchange recipes. Dinner was a time for talking, laughing, and sharing stories as well as eating. Now I couldn't do any of those!

I hadn't actually wanted to get a feeding g-tube at all. I figured I wouldn't need it until I was in my final days anyway. But with Bulbar Onset ALS, all loss of mouth functions were the first functions to go. My family convinced me to get a g-tube and I'm so grateful now. I got my supply of liquid formula, and I actually had an increase in energy. Without that nutrition, I would have missed our golden wedding anniversary, our grandson's wedding, and the birth of a new baby grandson. Still, I lament the fact that I'll never eat anything by mouth again. What could I do except turn to Jesus? As the Word of God told me, He is my Bread of Life.

Prayer

Lord Jesus, You taught us to pray, "Give us this day our daily bread." You must have meant more than that delicious crusty homemade bread I used to bake. Heavenly Father, You gave thousands of people manna in the wilderness. You taught them:

> Man does not live on bread alone but on every word that comes from the mouth of the Lord. (Deuteronomy 8:3b)

Jesus, You even quoted that verse. You fed Your people. You taught them. You spoke of Yourself as the Bread of Life. That's what I need now, the Bread of Life. You are what I need now! Only You can satisfy my true hunger. When I get angry and hungry for real food, please help me rely on You as my Bread of Life—Amen.

Jesus is the Bread of Life

Matthew 15 gives us a brief closeup of the compassion of Jesus, our Bread of Life. Jesus had just been in Bethsaida, grieving the brutal death of his relative John the Baptist, then teaching and feeding the 5,000. Now He was in Capernaum, on the other side of the lake, teaching 4,000. Jesus gathered His closest friends together to hear His plans in advance.

> Jesus called his disciples to him and said, "I have compassion for these people; they have already been with me three days

10

and have nothing to eat. I do not want to send them away hungry, or they may collapse on the way." (Matthew 15:32)

Each phrase of this verse has great meaning for us:

Jesus called his disciples to him and said... Wouldn't we all like to be that close to God that He would call us together to confide in us, and explain things to us? I often ask God, "Why?" and "What's next?" Sometimes I get an inkling of God's will through prayer, talking things over with other believers, and looking for God's hand in my life. But does my heart-desire to hear His voice send me longingly into His Word every single day? Is Jesus calling me close to Him to tell me something just as He did with His disciples? Yes, I think so.

I have compassion for these people... I love that about Jesus, that He was so compassionate! Imagine how exhausted Jesus must have been after preaching for three days! He was probably standing while they sat on the surrounding hills. Or maybe He was walking among them healing their sick. He always thought of them before Himself. I think of how God is concerned about us on our journeys. He's always looking at me with eyes of compassion and mercy, knowing what I'll encounter, and wanting to provide for me.

They have already been with me three days, and have nothing to eat... Certainly, the crowd hadn't planned to stay and listen to Jesus for three days! How long had it been since they ran out of food? Can you imagine receiving what seemed to be an empty basket, only to lift the napkin and find more food? More than 4,000 people took bread from the baskets—and they took all that they wanted! Jesus must have been delighted to see His people so satisfied by the food He gave them. There must have been a contagious joy within the crowd also, as they realized what was happening. And what hunger for truth they had! Do I have such hunger today?

11

Too often, I focus on my needs rather than on "knowing God."

I do not want to send them away hungry, or they may collapse on the way... Jesus will not send anyone away empty. Jesus not only fed this second multitude physically, but He fed them spiritually with His words.

The Gospel of John tells us that this is when Jesus explained Himself as the Bread of Life—maybe the most baffling of His names in the Bible. Jesus began by saying:

> Do not work for food that spoils, but for food that endures to eternal life, which the Son of Man will give you. (John 6:27)

Jesus had piqued their curiosity. They wondered what work they had to do to get food that would never run out, food that would be everlasting. Jesus then answered:

> The work of God is this: to believe in the one he has sent. (John 6:29)

So, Jesus made it clear that the work required to gain everlasting food is faith—faith in the One that God had sent, that is—faith in Jesus Himself. Jesus was explaining that He is the One whom God had sent and believing in Him is what matters.

> For the bread of God is the bread that comes down from heaven and gives life to the world." ³⁴"Sir," they said, "always give us this bread." ³⁵Then Jesus declared, "I am the bread of life. Whoever comes to me will never go hungry, and whoever believes in me will never be thirsty. (John 6:33-35)

Some doubted what He had to say, so Jesus promised four times that He would "raise up on the last day" whoever believes in Him. (John 6:39,40,44,54) With each new assertion, Jesus added a new depth of meaning, until He said:

> I am the living bread that came down from heaven. Whoever eats this bread will live forever. This bread is my flesh, which I will give for the life of the world. (John 6:51)

But for many skeptics, that was the "last straw!" Eating His body? That analogy was way too much to grasp. How can this man give us his flesh to eat? (John 6:52) So, many turned away from Him.

Jesus must have known that His words could make some people feel uncomfortable. The challenge of faith was difficult. He then turned to His twelve beloved, and asked what they thought. Simon Peter answered Him.

> Lord, to whom shall we go? You have the words of eternal life. 69We have come to believe and to know that you are the Holy One of God. (John 6:68b-69)

What the disciples didn't understand at the time was that Jesus would truly give His body for the forgiveness of our sins. Luke records what happened later at the last supper that Jesus ate with His disciples.

> And He took bread, gave thanks and broke it, and gave it to them, saying, "This is my body given for you; do this in remembrance of me." 20In the same way, after the supper He took the cup, saying, "This cup is the new covenant in my blood, which is poured out for you." (Luke 22:19-20)

How the disciples must have been puzzled by these words! At this time, they were oblivious to the meaning of His body being given and His blood poured out.

Today, we commemorate the Lord's Supper in communion. We understand that Jesus was willing to give His life, His death, and His blood shed on the cross to pay the price for our sins. We confess our own sinfulness, and accept that Jesus lovingly gave of Himself so that we might have forgiveness. We gladly receive Jesus' life into ours, just as we might gladly eat a piece of bread. We, who whole-heartedly believe in Jesus, have the promise of being raised up on the last day. Eternal life—the joyful result of accepting Jesus as the Bread of Life.

pALS Application

We pALS know we may not have long to live on this earth. During these final years, we might not even be able to eat food. But we can let our physical desire for food remind us that we can hunger for the Bread of Life.

Studying Jesus, as the Bread of Life, reveals Him as so likeable and engaging. He is unselfish and compassionate even when He Himself is so exhausted. He is always giving, always satisfying our spiritual hunger. He cares for us, His people, in miraculous ways. He can be trusted to give us what we need on a daily basis. And when He provides, there is always more than enough! His bread is the heavenly food that the Father gives through Him, and it comes with an everlasting promise.

We may wonder what lies ahead, what the future holds, and even whether God has been paying attention to our needs or our cries for help. But as we trust in Jesus, our Bread of Life, no matter how our disease progresses, Jesus will fill us with Himself. He will satisfy our hunger and our greatest longings...to live forever...with Him in heaven. Putting our faith in Jesus will gain us eternal life.

Closing Prayer

Lord Jesus, thank You for offering to fill me with Yourself. I want to come to You and be fed by You, the Bread of Life.

I love seeing how You revealed more of Yourself as You walked on this earth. I am so grateful that, even in Your tired, grieving body, You put others ahead of Yourself. You took time to teach Your people and free us from misunderstandings. You revealed truth to us. You are the rescuer of desperate and hurting people. You forgive us. You don't want to send people away to find our own provisions because You are our provider. You sustain us. You not only provide for many immediate temporal needs, but Your body and blood provide our eternal life.

Thank You that You are my Savior. You not only forgive me, but You give me joy and hope—no matter what my present physical state may be. I trust Your promise that You will raise me up on the last day because I believe in You. I long to live with You forever in eternity—Amen.

Reflections on Jesus as the Bread of Life

1. Do you long for Jesus to fill you as much as you used to long for food? What are you hungry for right now?

2. What does it mean to you that Jesus said He is the Bread of Life? If you cannot take communion anymore (i.e., cannot eat bread or swallow grape juice anymore), how do you think Jesus wants you to celebrate Him as the Bread of Life?

3. Why would Jesus ask that communion be done in remembrance of Him? (*See* Luke 22:19b) What do you remember best about Jesus when you celebrate communion?

4. John 6 (the chapter in which Jesus refers to Himself as the Bread of Life) is filled with references to believers being raised up on the last day, and living forever. Do these promises speak to you now? How do they help you face ALS?

3. Loss of Drinking Ability – Jesus is the Giver of Living Water

Be rightly related to God, find your joy there, and out of you will flow rivers of living water.—Oswald Chambers [5]

The Loss of Drinking Ability

My loss of the ability to swallow liquids followed my loss of the ability to swallow food by mouth. For a while, I could still swallow soups and favorite beverages, even if I had to "guzzle" them, feeling like a drunken spring-break college student I'd seen on the news. For me, the refreshing sensation of gulping some orange juice or iced caramel latte was such a delight—until rather suddenly, without warning, my throat totally stopped working. I experienced total dysphagia, swallowing spasms, and choking with repeated gulping noises until I'd lose my breath. The only thing that helped me when choking was putting my head between my knees and back-slapping.

Other crazy embarrassing symptoms ensued, because I couldn't even swallow my own saliva. During the day, I used a "drool cloth" or silicone bib. At night, I needed propped-up pillows, a suction device, a tongue scraper, and a sponge swab. I tried medications and various techniques, but I'd totally lost my ability to swallow anything. The loss of swallowing ability was my third functional loss, but it was taking its place as my #1 worst loss! And whenever I'd feel thirsty, there was oddly no way to quench my thirst—except through a feeding tube attached to my stomach.

Prayer

Lord, I am thirsty! Quenching my thirst by a tube feeding just isn't satisfying. I need a real drink! My mouth is becoming more and more useless—first no speech, then no eating, and now no drinking! How can I survive this awful loss? I have too much saliva, yet I can't swallow anything. How is this something that can possibly bring You glory when I'm a slobbering woman? I want more to life than this! I know I need YOU! Again, what can I do but turn to Your Word for help?

Lord, You bring to my mind another couple of verses from the Gospel of John. Jesus, You said:

> Let anyone who is thirsty come to me and drink. 38Whoever believes in me, as Scripture has said, rivers of living water will flow from within them. (John 7:37-38)

I want to be able to drink, but You are showing me that the drink You have for me is not of this world. It is a drink that can satisfy me emotionally and spiritually, bringing me peace and assurance of Your eternal love. Help me, Lord, to come to You and drink—Amen.

Jesus Gives Us Living Water

I love the story of Jesus talking about living water during His encounter with a Samaritan woman in John 4. Jesus had left Jerusalem with His disciples on His way to Galilee. After a twenty mile or so journey, He was weary and thirsty, so He stopped to rest near a well. As a Samaritan woman approached, Jesus asked her for a drink from the well and the story began.

Jesus had broken the cultural rules. Samaritans were despised outcasts from the Israelites, because their ancestors had abandoned the Jerusalem temple, preferring to set up their own temple, their own priests, and their own laws. By this time, their intermarriage with pagan foreigners had further corrupted their worship. So, when Jesus asked her for a favor, the Samaritan woman immediately replied:

> You are a Jew and I am a Samaritan woman. How can you ask me for a drink? (For Jews do not associate with Samaritans). (John 4:9)

Jesus then answered:

> If you knew the gift of God and who it is that asks you for a drink, you would have asked him and he would have given you living water. (John 4:10).

She must have been puzzled by His statement, so He went on to explain that the well water would never completely quench anyone's thirst.

> But whoever drinks the water I give them will never thirst. Indeed, the water I give them will become in them a spring of water welling up to eternal life. 15The woman said to him, "Sir, give me this water so that I won't get thirsty and have to keep coming here to draw water." (John 4:14-15)

That was a practical response to which Jesus may have smiled, so He decided to pursue the conversation further. Jesus brought up some questions about her home life. He gave her a test of truth. Go, call your husband. (John 4:16a) And then she spoke the truth, I have no husband. (John 4:17a) He congratulated her on her humble honesty. She perceived Jesus as a Prophet, because He knew the truth that she'd been married five times and was now living with someone.

Maybe she was embarrassed, so she changed the subject to discuss worship. Jesus told her that those who worship God ...must worship in spirit and truth. (John 4:24) There it was again—truth! Then the woman questioned Him about the Messiah. Jesus replied, I who speak to you am He! (John 4:26)

It was finally enough for her! She was amazed! After all her questions, she was convinced. She had heard the truth! She had heard the truth about her husbands and her current partner, the truth about worship, and the truth about Jesus' identity! So she left her waterpot at the well, and ran to tell her neighbors what she had learned.

> Come, see a man who told me everything I ever did. Could this be the Messiah? (John 4:29)

Jesus had broken the norms in speaking to this woman. But her physical and spiritual thirst for truth had brought her to believing in Jesus as the Messiah. The living water that Christ gave her was the truth. And it was already springing up in her to affect others. Her thirst had been quenched and now living water was overflowing to the people around her. Her testimony had become like a bubbling fountain of water, splashing all over her neighbors.

A few verses later, John wrote that many of the Samaritans of that city had become believers ...because of the woman's testimony. (John 4:39) Now all these people of her village were having *their* thirst quenched by believing in Jesus. Her thirst had been quenched. She even left her waterpot at the well!

Jesus and His disciples stayed at the village two more days and many more believed because of His word. The story concludes with this:

> They said to the woman, "We no longer believe just because of what you said; now we have heard for ourselves, and we know that this man really is the Savior of the world." (John 4:42)

What an amazing change had occurred in these Samaritan people. They had been downtrodden and despised. But now they were people who recognized that Jesus had come to save the world! They had received the truth and it was now pouring out of their mouths to others. What a joy it was for them—and what a joy it is for us—to know the Lord, the fountain of living waters!

We Can Share the Living Water

A spring of living water not only quenches our own thirst, it overflows to others. Like the Samaritan woman, our quenched thirst can result in a sparkling fountain of joy to be shared. Are you familiar with the story of Corrie ten Boom, who had tried to save the Jews from persecution during World War II? Eventually, she herself wound up in a concentration camp. Corrie later wrote a book called "The Hiding Place" in which she reflected on the sufferings of this world.

> *The world is deathly ill. It is dying. The Great Physician has already signed the death certificate. Yet, there is still a great work for Christians to do. They are to be streams of living water, channels of mercy to those who are still in the world. It is possible for them to do this because they are overcomers.* [6]

Oswald Chambers wrote something similar as he ministered to troops during World War I. He served as a chaplain stationed in Cairo, Egypt, a semi-desert city, located along the Nile River.

A river reaches places which its source never knows. And Jesus said that if we have received His fullness, 'rivers of living water' will flow out from us, reaching in blessing even 'to the end of the earth' regardless of how small the visible effects of our lives may appear to be. We have nothing to do with the outflow...God rarely allows a person to see how great a blessing he is to others. [7]

Both of these Christians knew that God's living water is meant to be shared. God often allows people to be thirsty, so that they can show others where the water is to be found.

pALS Application

Many of us are thirsty, yet unable to drink. We feel such frustration when we cannot even sip a taste of our favorite beverages anymore. Do we also have such a thirst for God? To those of us who are so thirsty—physically, emotionally, or spiritually—can we, like the Samaritan woman, leave our waterpots at the well and go straight to Jesus, the source of living water? Jesus, the living water, can quench our thirst and overflow into the lives of others.

I know it doesn't seem possible that we pALS could do that. We may feel more like the Samaritan woman, looked down upon as we slobber with our dysfunctional mouths. We may, in fact, feel powerless. But there is still great work for us to do as long as we are alive. I used to think of my "bucket list" to enjoy before I would be ready for hospice, but now I think of "God's bucket list for me." Who knows what He yet has in store for me to do? How does He want to live in and through me right now? How does He want me to be a stream of living water, a channel of mercy to a thirsty world right now?

Closing Prayer

Heavenly Father, I am so thirsty. I thirst for water, and I thirst for Your Living Water. Please take my eyes off my limitations and onto You. You have satisfied my every need in the past, and I know You will continue to surprise me with Your goodness and mercy.

I think of those who don't know You. Would You let Your Living Water flow through me to others? Would you let Your streams of mercy and goodness, love and forgiveness flow to all those who need You? You are our Provider —Amen.

Reflections on Jesus as the Giver of Living Water

1. What does it mean to you to be thirsty for God?

2. Are you thirstier for the ability to drink the beverages of this world, or for the Living Water that Jesus gives? How does the promise of Living Water give you hope?

3. Have you ever felt the joy of His Living Water splashing into your life? Describe it.

4. The Samaritan woman recognized the Living Water as truth. Corrie ten Boom recognized the Living Water as channels of mercy. How can you let Jesus' Living Water of truth and mercy splash into another's life?

4. Loss of Connections – Jesus is the Vine

Why do bad things happen to good people? That only happened once and He volunteered. —R. C. Sproul [8]

The Loss of Connections

After my first few bulbar symptoms, I realized that I could lose connections with some friends. I couldn't talk, and I hadn't yet gotten used to my speech app. I needed to proofread everything I typed on my app before I played it, or I'd be in trouble. "Auto-correct" once caused me to swear at a friend, and when I thought I had typed "honey dear" to my brilliant daughter, it came out "dummy head!" We can laugh now, but incorrect "auto-corrects" were such an embarrassment.

Going out anywhere became difficult. Driving at night became more difficult. In fact, driving anywhere began to fatigue me. I didn't want to miss out on gatherings of friends, family, our weekly Bible study women's group, our fall apple-picking, and pumpkin-patch hayrides. The COVID pandemic and quarantines also added to the frustrations. As my grandkids would say, my FOMO—fear of missing out—would kick in.

So the Lord would remind me to write in my gratitude journal about my many caring supporters. I began to realize that a lot of those caring friends were people who were also connected to Jesus. They would pray, bring food (while I could still eat), send gifts, and cards (stacked so deep now that I have to keep finding new boxes and baskets in which to store them!)

But I realize that it's not like that for every one of my pALS. In various Facebook groups, online Zoom groups, and webinars, I hear of pALS who are lonely and depressed. Some pALS have friends who've lost others to ALS. Then those friends quietly slipped out of their lives, unwilling to face the decline and loss of another person with ALS. Some pALS have neighbors who offered to help, but then they didn't know what to do, and became busy with their own lives. Some pALS have caregivers with whom they have trouble relating. Some pALS have people who offered to visit but never showed up. Loneliness and depression can set into pALS without notice.

Prayer

Heavenly Father, You know we humans need a sense of belonging. You created us to love You and love one another. It can get so hard when we do not sense Your love or the love of others. You do not want us to be alone. Father God, You have said that You are with us. Jesus Himself told us that He will always be with us. We often sense Your presence as we pray and meditate on Your Word. But we need people, too.

We need people who will be near us—not only caregivers for our weary bodies but also people to be near to our hearts. We need people who understand our emotional needs, our spiritual needs, our relational needs, our need for love. Please help us, Heavenly Father, to realize that You are here with us each day, and that You are at work in the world around us. Please bring us closer to You and let us experience more of the love of Your Son Jesus and the fullness of Your Spirit. When we feel we are lacking earthly friends, would You please put us on the hearts of those who know You? Would You please help us stay connected to others who know You? More importantly, would You please help us stay closely connected to You?—Amen.

Jesus is the Vine

In John 15, Jesus gives another explanation of who He is:

I am the vine; you are the branches. If you remain in me and I in you, you will bear much fruit; apart from me you can do nothing... ⁹As the Father loved Me, I also have loved you; abide in My love. ¹⁰If you keep My commandments, you will abide in My love, just as I have kept My Father's commandments and abide in His love. ¹¹These things I have spoken to you, that My joy may remain in you, and that your joy may be full. ¹²This is My commandment, that you love one another as I have loved you. (John 15:5,9-12 NKJV)

Abiding, dwelling, living in and remaining in Jesus—that's the answer to our sense of belonging. He provides the sense of connection we so want in our lives. We stay connected to Jesus because He is the strong healthy Vine. As we grow, like shoots off the Vine, we find ourselves surrounded by other branches, other believers also connected to Him. In John 15:12, noted above, Jesus tells us to love one another. And in verse 15, He says: I have called you friends. (*See* John 15:15) That is so amazing to be a friend of Jesus!

One of my favorite stories about Jesus' friendships while He was on the earth concerns three siblings: Martha, Mary, and Lazarus. When Jesus was near Jerusalem, He was a frequent visitor at their home in Bethany. The first time we read about His visit is when Martha worked to serve Him, but Mary sat at His feet (*See* Luke 10:38-42). Later we hear that Mary poured perfume on Him and wiped His feet with her hair during a dinner at their house (*See* John 11:2). And then later, we hear that Lazarus became ill. The sisters sent word to Jesus. *Lord, the one you love is sick.* (John 11:3) It pained Jesus not to be there, but, a few days later, He was able to show His connection to Lazarus with the most power and love.

When Jesus and His disciples arrived in Bethany, they found Lazarus had already died and had rested in the tomb for four days. Many of the Jews had come to comfort Mary and Martha on the death of their brother. The introverted thinker Martha went out to meet Jesus on the road, and stated perhaps rather matter-of-factly, *Lord, if you had been here, my brother would not have died.* (John 11:21b) She continued with thoughtful respect, *But I know that even now God will give you whatever you ask.* (John 11:22)

Jesus promised that Lazarus would rise again, and Martha stated she knew that. But she was concerned about the here-and-now! Jesus challenged her faith a bit further, and told her:

> *I am the resurrection and the life. The one who believes in me will live, even though they die; 26and whoever lives by believing in me will never die. Do you believe this?* (John 11:25-26)

Perhaps no one had ever been this direct with Martha. She responded with what she believed:

> *I believe that you are the Messiah, the Son of God, who is to come into the world.* (John 11:27)

That was an astounding confession of faith. Some disciples had said He might be "the Messiah," or "the Holy One of God," or a "Prophet". Martha strongly professed her own faith by calling Him the Messiah and the Son of God!

It was also astounding how Jesus met Martha right where she was—intellectually, emotionally, and spiritually. Jesus knew that Martha would actually be comforted by openly stating her faith in Him. Perhaps even Martha was surprised when she heard the words come out of her mouth! Such a profession of faith was just what she needed. Those words taught her to profess truth, gaining God's perspective on what had just happened and what was to come. She didn't say any more to Jesus at this time, but rushed back to get her sister Mary, saying "the Teacher" was there for her.

The more extroverted Mary had been in the house grieving with her friends. She rushed out to meet Jesus. Her greeting was the same as her sister's: Lord, if you had been here, my brother would not have died. (John 11:32) But Mary then fell at His feet weeping. Her friends were there with her weeping as well. Jesus was overwhelmed, troubled and deeply moved in His spirit, asking only where they had laid him. Then He wept too. Mary's friends even said of Jesus, See how he loved him! (John 11:36)

Jesus was so connected relationally to this family. One sister needed an intellectual challenge to help her grow in faith and understand the meaning of the resurrection of the body. The other sister needed the emotional support of someone to cry with her. Jesus was right there with them, loving them. He wanted to demonstrate that love even further. He went to the grave and asked people to roll away the stone. After a prayer, Jesus called, Lazarus, come forth! (John 11:43) And Lazarus rose from the dead, and many more people now believed.

pALS Application

While we pALS may be nearing death as Lazarus was, Jesus calls us to come to Him. He could call us to come to Him for healing in this temporary life, or to come to Him for eternity. The important thing is to come—to be connected to Him as the Vine, and be related to the other branches.

> All those the Father gives me will come to me, and whoever comes to me I will never drive away. (John 6:37)

> I am the way, the truth, and the life. No one comes to the Father except through Me. (John 14:6)

Coming to Jesus makes us part of God the Father's family, accepted in the Beloved as stated in Ephesians 1:6 (NKJV). We belong to God's family in heaven, and His family on earth. At times when I have needed the emotional and spiritual support of friends, another believer will call, email, text, or send a card—it might even be from a social media friend, or a friend from another state! I can't help but feel that it is a "divine appointment" and "God-coincidence" (or "God-incidence" as our Pastor Hanibal Rodriguez would say [9]). It's not really a coincidence that "It just so happened that…" It is part of God's sovereignty and love for us. We will always have the love of Christ as part of His family.

> Who shall separate us from the love of Christ? Shall tribulation, or distress, or persecution, or famine, or nakedness, or peril, or sword? [36]As it is written:

> "For Your sake we are killed all day long; We are accounted as sheep for the slaughter."

> [37]Yet in all these things we are more than conquerors through Him who loved us. [38]For I am persuaded that neither death nor life, nor angels nor principalities nor powers, nor things present nor things to come, [39]nor height nor depth, nor any other created thing, shall be able to separate us from the love of God which is in Christ Jesus our Lord. (Romans 8:35-39)

Jesus loves us as much as God His Father loves Him! And Jesus said He told us these things so that we would have His joy—a full measure of it!

Is a sense of belonging and a full measure of joy still possible for pALS? Jesus says, "Yes!"—I have called you friends. (John 15:15)

Closing Prayer

Heavenly Father, thank You that You want me to belong to You. Thank You for securing a place for me in your Vine. You have not only given me joy in belonging to Your community of faith on this earth—You have provided a family for me in heaven. You have adopted me as Your child, and Jesus even calls me His friend. You have made me accepted in the Beloved. (Ephesians 1:6b NKJV) I worship You as God Almighty and Everlasting. May I experience Your love forever—Amen.

Reflections on Jesus as the Vine

1. Have you suffered the loss of any friends or favorite connections since you were diagnosed with ALS? Do you feel lonely or isolated? Have you talked to God about that?

2. How has Jesus showed you His friendship and love in recent months?

3. How have other believers (other branches on the Vine) shown you their friendship?

4. Meditate on what it means to belong to God. Write your own prayer of gratitude for the relationship you have with God.

5. Loss of Accomplishments—Jesus is the Giver of Fruit of His Spirit

It is the evidence of the fruit of the Spirit that is the mark of our progress in sanctification. Of course, God is pleased when we dutifully exercise the gifts the Holy Spirit has bestowed upon us. But I think God is even more pleased when He sees His people manifest the fruit of the Spirit.—R.C. Sproul [10]

The Loss of Accomplishments

Along with my loss of functions, I felt I was also experiencing the loss of accomplishments. I'm retired but I wanted to keep setting exciting goals and objectives for myself. But the truth was, I couldn't. I felt that my goals had diminished to managing my symptoms and taking my medications.

One by one, I had to resign from my former activities, service roles, and volunteer work. I'd led a Bible study small group and served as a coach, but I found that God had prepared other amazing women to take my place. I stayed involved in a core leadership role, but only as long as I could easily endure long meetings and talk through my iPad speech app.

In my neighborhood, I'd been an active volunteer, but soon I was relegated to merely stuffing envelopes. I'd enjoyed gardening, crafts with my grandkids, sewing, woodburning, watercolor painting, but my energy was flagging. I began scheduling only one daily activity besides my daily nap. I'd try to stay awake and motivated to write texts, emails, and notes to friends. But sometimes a "brain fog" would call me to an unplanned nap. Maybe it was the medications' side effects; maybe it was just ALS fatigue; but my life was changing in ways I certainly didn't like!

Prayer

Oh, Lord, I know that my value is not based on what I can accomplish in life. I know that it's an insult to You to even think I can earn Your favor by performing for You. But I'm feeling like my value has diminished, as I'm not very useful to anyone anymore. Help me, Lord, to know what to do about my loss of accomplishments.

(*I have prayed that prayer a lot. Then one day, the Lord reminded me of His name as the Vine. It doesn't matter if we can no longer accomplish what we used to—Jesus grows the grapes on our branches as long we stay connected to Him. That changed the tone of my prayer.*)

Lord, I want to enjoy being a branch on your grapevine. I just want to abide in You, and see how You may cause fruit to develop from the branches of my withered arms. Jesus, I remember You said that we can't bear fruit on our own. We have to be connected to You. And that it will be to Your Father's glory that we bear fruit and show that we are Your disciples.

(*The Lord also brought to my mind that I'd been a part of His grapevine for a long time. I've had wonderfully supportive and encouraging relationships with "other branches" on His Vine. I'd been grateful for them for years, and now I realized that it was all from God. It was all of His good timing and His good plan. Just as they had supported me, I realized that now, my journaling on the topics of ALS losses might be helpful to other pALS. While I lament my losses, the Lord has given me a more relevant understanding of Jesus to comfort me. I began to overflow with joy, and I knew I couldn't keep it to myself.*)

Praise be to the God and Father of our Lord Jesus Christ, the Father of compassion and the God of all comfort, [4]who comforts us in all our troubles, so that we can comfort those in any trouble with the comfort we ourselves receive from God. (2Corinthians 1:3-4)

(I realized God had given me a new "bucket list" goal—to write a devotional for pALS, based on Jesus as "A Living Savior". Even as I struggled with my own loss of accomplishments, I began to research "fruit" in the Bible.)

But the fruit of the Spirit is love, joy, peace, forbearance, kindness, goodness, faithfulness, [23]gentleness and self-control. Against such things there is no law. [24]Those who belong to Christ Jesus have crucified the flesh with its passions and desires. [25]Since we live by the Spirit, let us keep in step with the Spirit. [26]Let us not become conceited, provoking and envying each other. (Galatians 5:22-25)

Lord Jesus, I know that You've given me more than the goal of writing a devotional—You want to give me the fruit of Your Spirit. That means I need to confess my old selfish desires, and trust You to keep me in step with Your Spirit. That means I will let go of pride, arguing, and envying others who are doing better than I am. Lord, please help me. Help other pALS. We all need to see Your fruit in our lives—Amen.

Jesus Gives us His Spirit for Fruit in our Lives

After Jesus sent His Spirit upon believers at Pentecost, stories about the fruit of the Spirit abound in the book of Acts. I especially love the stories of the early church women, one of my favorites being Lydia. She was a dealer in purple cloth, the color of royalty, priestly garments, and coincidently, a favorite color of mine (and the color of my wedding attendants, a separate story!) Lydia would probably be a great friend and role model for me today, as she met with a group of women to pray by the riverside outside of Philippi. That's where Paul and Silas joined them to pray and preach about Jesus.

One day, a slave woman/fortune-teller kept bothering the group, so Paul and Silas cast the demon out of her. The woman's owners were angry because they would no longer have income from her psychic powers. They led the town in a protest And soon Paul and Silas were stripped, beaten, and thrown into prison. Their pain intensified as they had to sit in an agonizing position with their feet in stocks. But the astounding thing was that they started praying and singing hymns to God, and the other prisoners were listening to them. (Acts 16:25b)

What happened next was fantastic! An earthquake opened the prison doors and their chains fell off! The jailer thought that the prisoners had escaped, so he was about to kill himself, maybe because he feared an even more brutal punishment from his supervisors. But just as he was about to end his life, Paul exclaimed, Don't harm yourself! We are all here! (Acts 16:28b)

The jailer then called for lights, and could see that Paul and Silas had not escaped. Perhaps they even continued singing **joyful** praise to God. They were **peaceful, patient, and longsuffering** in their imprisonment. How could that be possible? They had shown **goodness** to the jailer, not letting him proceed with killing himself, and **kindness** in letting him know that all the prisoners were still there. They could have quickly escaped, but **self-control** urged them to stay and speak with the distraught jailer.

What happened next was even more fantastic! The jailer fell trembling before Paul and Silas, and asked:

"Sirs, what must I do to be saved?"... 31[Paul and Silas] replied: "Believe in the Lord Jesus, and you will be saved—you and your household." (Acts 16:29b,31)

The jailer humbly agreed. He took them to his household and washed their wounds as Paul and Silas **gently** spoke the Word of the Lord to him. The jailer and his household believed and were baptized. And they too began to show more of the fruit of the Spirit. The jailer set a meal before them with **love and kindness**, and was filled with joy because he had come to believe in God—he and his whole household. (Acts 16:34)

The next day Paul, a Roman citizen, spoke to the magistrates about his rights that had been violated. Paul showed his **faithfulness** not only to God but also to his fellow citizens in defending their rights. Then he showed **faithfulness** to the other Christians who met at Lydia's house, encouraging them before he left.

So much fruit of the Spirit is evident in this one story! How did Paul and Silas get to the point of rejoicing and praising God when they were in jail?—especially with their bloody backs and their feet in stocks! Would I have been singing praises at a time like that? I doubt it! They had a lot more character than I do! They had already endured so much on their missionary travels. On their first trip, Paul had been stoned, left for dead, and dragged out of the city of Lystra. Certainly, their faith had been tested.

James says, You know that the testing of your faith produces perseverance. 4Let perseverance finish its work so that you may be mature and complete, not lacking anything. (James 1:3b-4)

But that leaves us with some questions: Exactly how does perseverance do its work, much less finish it? How does anyone get to the point of having so much fruit of the Spirit in their lives?

pALS Application

As a pALS, I definitely needed more insight into the work of perseverance. I found that Romans 5 tells us:

> We glory in our sufferings, because we know that **suffering** produces **perseverance**; [4]**perseverance, character; and character, hope.** [5]And hope does not put us to shame, because God's love has been poured out into our hearts through the Holy Spirit, who has been given to us. (Romans 5:3b-5, emphasis added)

These verses explain how perseverance actually produces fruit in our lives. It's a four-step process:

1. Suffering,

2. Perseverance,

3. Character, and

4. Hope (because the love of God is poured into our hearts by the Holy Spirit.)

So we may ask, "What step am I on?" We may assume that with ALS we are still at the suffering or perseverance point. But with each new trial, we can go through all four steps. With each new trial, we persevere, see more character being developed in our lives, feel more hope and the love of God in our hearts.

This may be the answer to experiencing the loss of our own accomplishments: *Abiding in the Vine* keeps us connected to Jesus and other believers. *Persevering through suffering* develops the beautiful fruit of character. *Seeing fruit in our lives* gives us hope. And then, just as Paul and Silas experienced, the Holy Spirit pours the love of God into our hearts.

And that hope and love of God enable us to persevere with each new bit of suffering. **We're not working on our own goals and accomplishments anymore.** We give them to Jesus and He gives us the fruit of His Spirit and the love of the Father. And that makes it—pure joy!

> Be filled with the Spirit, [19]speaking to one another with psalms, hymns, and songs from the Spirit. Sing and make music from your heart to the Lord, [20]always giving thanks to God the Father for everything, in the name of our Lord Jesus Christ. (Ephesians 5:18b-20)

Closing Prayer

Heavenly Father, thank You that You cause fruit to grow in my life. The last thing I would have thought is that I would be fruitful during my disability!

God, how You work in miraculous ways!

Please grow Your fruit in me as I surrender my life to You. My physical life is falling apart, but I want to persevere in faith in You. Only You are able to fill me with **love and joy and peace** to extend to others. You help me have patience with my symptoms, **patience** with my friends and family, patience with my caregivers, patience with myself and my failures as I confess my sin to You. I'm unable to accomplish any usual goals, but help me to be **kind and good** to others, and **faithful** to You, Jesus.

Knowing You, Jesus, as gentle and humble in the midst of Your own suffering, reminds me to come to You every day.

As I rest in You, rather than in my own accomplishments, help me become like You in Your **gentleness**, putting others ahead of myself. Please grow humble **self-control** within me also, so that in all my days, I may bring glory to You—Amen.

Reflections on Jesus as the Giver of Fruit of His Spirit

1. The fruit of the Spirit is singular (not plural, "fruits"), and each attribute of the fruit is part of being transformed into Jesus' image. We may see one attribute (like kindness or gentleness) already evident in our lives, while one or more are still growing in our lives. Which attribute do you think God is growing in your life right now? (*See* Galatians 5:22 above.)

2. Jesus demonstrated all the fruit of the Spirit in His life. Which attribute of the fruit of the Sprit most attracts you to Him?

3. What is the main challenge to your perseverance now?

4. If you were to "sing and make music from your heart to the Lord," what words would you use? (*See* Ephesians 5:18-20 above)

6. Loss of Mobility – Jesus is the Good Shepherd

We are secure, not because we hold tightly to Jesus, but because He holds tightly to us.—R.C. Sproul [11]

> He tends his flock like a shepherd:
> He gathers the lambs in his arms
> and carries them close to his heart;
> He gently leads those that have young.
>
> (Isaiah 40:11)

Loss of Mobility

I am hurrying to complete my writing, before I have loss of my limbs. My hand and arm get tired after writing for about 20 minutes, and after that, my penmanship devolves into small unreadable scratches. But I can still type pretty well! And I'm still fairly active—driving, walking, sometimes swimming a bit (with a flotation device). Our daughter even caught my husband and me on video, wrapped in each other's arms, swaying together to some Christmas music. My shoulders, neck, back, and legs are always a bit stiff and easily fatigued, but they still work!

Loss of mobility is often part of the earlier symptoms of regular ALS, but for those of us with Bulbar Onset ALS, loss of mobility will likely be one of the last stages. I've started using a rollator (rolling walker), given to me by our daughter. Sometimes I want to know how long it will be until I collapse in a wheelchair. Sometimes I'd rather not know.

Prayer

Heavenly Father, you know the future. In this case, I'm fairly glad I don't. At this time, I want to keep enjoying my family and friends, and bringing glory to You. I'm growing more content to be moving to heaven soon, although I hate the thought of having to be carried anywhere on this earth. I don't want to be immobile! When the time comes, I will reach out to You and ask You to carry me through.

When I first came to know You, Jesus, it was your words of John 10 that spoke to my heart. You said You knew me by name and called me and gave me abundant life as part of Your flock. Yes, You are my Good Shepherd. You can carry me close to Your heart—Amen.

Jesus is our Good Shepherd

Scripture is full of references to God as our Shepherd, and Jesus Himself spoke about His own shepherding experience.

> I am the gate; whoever enters through me will be saved. They will come in and go out, and find pasture. [10]The thief comes only to steal and kill and destroy; I have come that they may have life, and have it to the full. [11]I am the good shepherd. The good shepherd lays down his life for the sheep. (John 10:9-11)

If we have entered into His flock, and are now "in Christ," He promised we will enjoy all the benefits of a full life. Psalm 94 speaks of His tender care.

> Unless the Lord had given me help,
>   I would soon have dwelt in the silence of death.
> [18]When I said, "My foot is slipping,"
>   your unfailing love, Lord, supported me.

[19]When anxiety was great within me,
  your consolation brought me joy. (Psalm 94:17-19)

Jesus is there for us, supporting us when our feet are slipping or our hearts are anxious. His Word in Deuteronomy has an all-encompassing verse that speaks great encouragement to us:

The eternal God is your refuge, and underneath are the everlasting arms. (Deuteronomy 33:27)

Another favorite story of mine concerns how Jesus interacted with Peter, a man in need of a Good Shepherd. Jesus first called "Simon Bar-Jonah" to follow Him, for as He said in John 10:3, He calls his own sheep by name and leads them out. Jesus then changed his name to Peter (meaning "rock"), indicating that he would have a rock-solid faith. Peter even showed that faith by walking on water toward Jesus. Matthew's Gospel tells us:

"Lord, if it's you," Peter replied, "tell me to come to you on the water." [29]"Come," [Jesus] said.

Then Peter got down out of the boat, walked on the water and came toward Jesus. [30]But when he saw the wind, he was afraid and, beginning to sink, cried out, "Lord, save me!"

[31]Immediately Jesus reached out his hand and caught him. "You of little faith," he said, "why did you doubt?" (Matthew 14:28-30)

Although Peter was not yet an example of a man with rock-solid faith, he clearly stated what he believed about Jesus: You are the Messiah, the Son of the living God. (Matthew 16:16) However, many of us have heard the "rooster crow" story about Peter, when he later denied that he even knew Jesus (*See* Matthew 26:34-75). Peter was a wayward sheep after all.

After Jesus' death and resurrection, we read in John 21 about how He reached out to Peter after that denial episode. Peter must have been so completely discouraged with himself, even after Jesus' resurrection. Jesus had appeared twice to the disciples, but they did not yet know what was to come. So, one morning, Peter and his friends went back to fishing (fishing for actual "fish," not for "men" as Jesus had said, for they had not yet completely understood what that meant).

After Jesus caused them to fill their nets, Peter went happily and humbly to greet Him. Peter must have been prepared for whatever rebuke Jesus might give him. How would the Good Shepherd confront Peter after his denial? A shepherd might beat him with His rod, or put His staff around his neck and yank him back into the fold. But Jesus had prepared a meal of grilled fish and bread for them. After breakfast, Jesus and Peter had a memorable conversation. Jesus began by asking Peter a question:

> When they had finished eating, Jesus said to Simon Peter, "Simon son of John, do you love me more than these?" "Yes, Lord," he said, "you know that I love you." Jesus said, "Feed my lambs." (John 21:15)

Although Jesus must have been disappointed with Peter's betrayal of Him, He didn't impose any guilt on him. Maybe to save Peter from embarrassment, Jesus used Peter's original name, Simon Bar-Jonah, without any shame for his failure to be a rock-solid believer.

"Do you love me more than these?" Peter answered that he loved the Lord dearly as a friend, but he humbly avoided comparing himself to the others. Jesus then repeated the question, leaving off any possible comparison between Peter's love for Him, and that of the disciples, or any other

46

possible comparison to Peter's love for any other person or thing in his life. Jesus simply asked the second question:

> "Simon son of John, do you love me?"
>
> [Peter] answered, "Yes, Lord, you know that I love you."
>
> Jesus said, "Take care of my sheep." (John 21:16)

Peter replied, understanding that Jesus knew his heart of repentance and love. Jesus then entrusted him with another responsibility of being a good shepherd—caring for the sheep, not merely feeding them. We already know from other Scriptures that God describes a good shepherd as one who supports and consoles his sheep. This is exactly what Jesus was doing here, caring for and consoling Peter, and passing that responsibility onto him for the future.

Jesus had asked twice whether Peter loved Him with an "agape love" (the unconditional, sacrificial love of God). *Peter, do you really love me with an unconditional love?* But he could only reply that he loved Jesus with tenderly brotherly affection. Peter knew in the depth of his own heart that his own emotions were often too fickle to pledge undying love. He was honest and open. Peter knew Jesus saw his heart, and that he was incapable of "agape love."

Jesus then proceeded kindly a third time, but this time He matched His inquiry to Peter's replies. Jesus re-phrased His question, using Peters' own words. He asked if Peter loved Him with a "phileo love" (a tender brotherly love, with a close bond of trust, affection and respect).

> The third time he said to him, "Simon son of John, do you love me?" Peter was hurt because Jesus asked him the third time, "Do you love me?" He said, "Lord, you know all things; you know that I love you." Jesus said, "Feed my sheep. (John 21:17)

Peter had already professed his brotherly love. Maybe at the time, Peter had wanted to put aside thoughts of his earlier days of abandoning Jesus. He may not have wanted to think about his earlier denial. Maybe he had just been enjoying his reunion with Jesus as they sat on the beach and ate grilled fish. Jesus was perhaps again laughing and smiling at his disciples. But then he startled Peter with some piercing questions that made Peter's heart jump.

Maybe it was all that and more that made Peter say, Lord, you know all things; you know that I love you. (*How could anyone not love You as a brother? I know my weaknesses and selfishness. You see my heart for what it is. You have forgiven me, and I am indebted to You. You know that I trust You and respect You. You know that I feel a close bond of tender affection for You. You know that I love You.*)

But maybe now, this third question sadly reminded Peter of his three denials and the "rooster crow." When bystanders asked Peter about his relationship with Jesus when He was on trial, Peter denied three times that he even knew Him. Now, he appreciated the forgiveness that Jesus offered him, professing his gratitude and love: Lord, you know all things; you know that I love you.

Jesus' responses to Peter revealed what a good shepherd does. Peter was pursued by the love of his Savior. While Peter had abandoned Jesus at His time of need, Jesus went after Peter in their conversation on the beach, carrying him back to the fold. Earlier, Jesus' parable had spoken about a wandering sheep: And when he finds it, he joyfully puts it on his shoulders ⁶and goes home. (Luke 15:5-6)

Looking back at his life, Peter knew what it was like to be carried by Jesus. When Peter walked on the water of the Sea of Galilee toward Jesus, Peter got fearful and almost slipped into the sea, but Jesus saved him. (*See* Matthew

14:31). Peter knew what it was like to be physically carried by Jesus's arms.

When Peter had denied Jesus three times, he fell into an appalling depth of sin. But, the chance to declare aloud three times that he loved Jesus gave him assurance of restoration. Peter had been spiritually carried by Jesus' arms of forgiveness.

When Peter was wondering what he would do next, Jesus told him to Feed my lambs, Take care of my sheep, and Feed my sheep. Peter was being taught to care for others, to become a good shepherd like his beloved master. In fact, brotherly love, in caring for one another, would identify the whole flock:

> By this everyone will know that you are my disciples if you love one another. (John 13:35)

Peter had experienced what it was like to be carried relationally by his Good Shepherd.

Finally, Jesus indicated that Peter would suffer a death of suffering, but He said once again, Follow Me! (*See* John 21:15-19) Peter would be eternally carried by Jesus into a redeemed life.

pALS Application

pALS can find it easy to relate to being a lame sheep. It's more than just needing someone to carry us physically. Jesus wants to carry us emotionally. Jesus wants to carry us spiritually. Jesus wants to carry us relationally. Jesus wants to hear me say I love Him and let Him take care of me as a Good Shepherd would want to do.

And Jesus also wants us, even us pALS, to help Him feed His sheep. There are other sheep who need His help, and need feeding. And we remember that Jesus feeds us through His Word, His Bread of Life, Himself.

Closing Prayer

Jesus, my Good Shepherd, I trust You to carry me through all the rough terrain of this life, feeding me on Your Word, nurturing me with Your love, and shepherding me home. Thank You that You carry me through my need for forgiveness, through my need for hope, through my need for eternity with You—Amen.

Reflections on Jesus as the Good Shepherd

1. If Jesus asked if you loved Him, how would you respond?

2. In which way do you need to rest in the arms of your Good Shepherd now—physically, emotionally, spiritually, relationally? Ask Him for His help.

3. Are you aware of any lost sheep in your life? What is Jesus calling you to do to help them be a part of His flock?

4. Write a prayer here (and on the next page as needed) to your Good Shepherd.

7. Loss of Breathing – Jesus is the Giver of the Breath of Life

Prayer is to the Christian what breath is to life, yet no duty of the Christian is so neglected. —R.C. Sproul [12]

Through Christ you can breathe again, inhaling the words of God that always surround you, exhaling word and deeds of praise that reflect all of who He is. —Louie Giglio [13]

The Loss of Breath

Thankfully, I have not yet lost my breathing ability. I get short of breath and easily fatigued doing ordinary activity, but my breathing scores are doing fairly well. I don't wear a CPAP or sleeping mask, but I think of those who wear a trilogy mask or a ventilator 24/7. Many are simply grateful for the technology that allows them to inhale and exhale. And we know it's not only ALS, but COVID, COPD and pneumonia that can lead to lung failure. But how horribly frustrating it must be to have entered that state! How I have compassion for those who are already at that point on their journey!

Prayer

Heavenly Father, I pray for those who are just surviving by breathing through some technical device. We look to You as our Breath of Life. You are the One who breathed life into the first human being, Adam. And now we rejoice when we see a newborn take his or her first breath of life after birth! Yet healthy people don't even think of breathing most of the time. It's just a normal activity that we take for granted.

So, Lord, may I say right now how grateful I am for every breath since birth. I love every bit of fresh air, every delicious aroma of food from cinnamon muffins and coffee, to steak on the grill, and chocolate fondues. I love scented shower gels, and fragrant sprays. I love the delicate hint of flowers as they bloom, and the faint whiff of candles as they glow. You have blessed us with so many delightful smells. I want to inhale Your goodness. Inhaling is such a delight!

And exhaling, getting more challenging now, is such a relief. I'm so grateful to breathe out the CO2 I don't need. I breathe out the bad thoughts, the frustration and anger. I breathe out the bad memories and choose to breathe out forgiveness to those who have hurt me. I need to breathe out the way I've hurt others too. I've never been so aware of what I am exhaling until now!

May I now use my exhaling for Your praise and adoration. I pray my breath and my praises of You will last as long as possible on this earth—Amen.

Jesus Gives us the Breath of Life

The Breath of Life is one of the first things we learn about in the Bible:

> Then the Lord God formed a man from the dust of the ground and breathed into his nostrils the breath of life, and the man became a living being. (Genesis 2:7)

For each of us, God is the source of life in all that we do. In our lifespan, we breathe approximately 700 million breaths—or 8 million breaths a year! Hard to grasp! 20,000 breaths a day. [14] Is that easier to grasp? All through Scripture are references to the breath that God gives us.

John's Gospel tells us, in chapter 20, about a very tangible encounter with the "breath of God." After Jesus' resurrection, He appeared to His disciples.

> On the evening of that first day of the week, when the disciples were together, with the doors locked for fear of the Jewish leaders, Jesus came and stood among them and said, "Peace be with you!" (John 20:19)

The disciples had been agitated and afraid of the Jewish leaders, so that's why Jesus started by saying, Peace be with you! Imagine someone who had just died a horrible death coming to life again! He had been dead, but now He was truly alive and breathing. Were they in awe at His being alive, or questioning reality? They could see his scarred features. Were they repulsed or ashamed of themselves for not having been there for Him? Jesus knew their troubled hearts. He drew them close and repeated,

> "Peace be with you!" as he showed them His hands and side. Again Jesus said, "Peace be with you! As the Father has sent me, I am sending you." 22And with that he breathed on them and said, "Receive the Holy Spirit. 23If you forgive anyone's sins, their sins are forgiven; if you do not forgive them, they are not forgiven." (John 20:21-23)

When He drew them close to Himself, He breathed on them, saying, Receive the Holy Spirit. They received the same breath that He had imparted originally to Adam, the same breath that fills every newborn's lungs—a breath of God. In addition, the disciples received a temporary experience of the Holy Spirit that Jesus promised they would receive in all His fullness at Pentecost (See Acts 2).

As Jesus breathed upon them at this time, the most important thing He said was about forgiveness. First, the disciples must have needed to forgive each other for envy and competition. After all, as recently as the Last Supper, hadn't they just been arguing who was the greatest among them? (*See* Luke 22:24).

They also needed to forgive those who had opposed Jesus. That included the Pharisees and Romans who had just crucified their friend Jesus. If the disciples would hold onto fear and hatred for Jesus' enemies, it would be difficult to advance His kingdom. Jesus' kingdom would include **all** who would put their faith in Him, even those who had formerly persecuted Him.

The disciples might also have needed to forgive any family members who berated them for following Jesus (*See* Luke 12:52-53). And, they must have needed, as we might say today, to "forgive themselves" by refusing to cling to the guilt and shame of their own lives. The Holy Spirit would guide them in confessing sin, accepting forgiveness from Jesus, and living a new life in Him. Then they would be able to preach the very good news of the Messiah, the Savior, Jesus, and be able to promise God's forgiveness to all those who believed in Him.

As we apply this to ourselves, we can realize what we need to do. While we have breath, can we forgive all who have hurt us in this life? While we have breath, can we resolve to avoid evil, as Job said:

> As long as I have life within me, the breath of God in my nostrils, 4my lips will not say anything wicked, and my tongue will not utter lies. (Job 27:3-4)

While we have breath, we can also now assure others of God's forgiveness. When Jesus breathed the Holy Spirit on the disciples, He knew that His Spirit would bring them new insight—Jesus' suffering on the cross was the atoning sacrifice for the sins of the world. R.C. Sproul put it this way: "If you take away the cross as an atoning act, you take away Christianity." [15]

Jesus had just died on the cross, accepting the wrath of God against the sins of all mankind, so that those who repented and put their faith in Him would be forgiven. After the disciples later received the fullness of the Holy Spirit, they understood the atonement, repented, and put their trust in Jesus. Now they were able to go into the world, sharing that message, and telling others how to receive God's forgiveness.

Matthew's Gospel concludes with these words:

> Then Jesus came to them and said, "All authority in heaven and on earth has been given to me. [19]Therefore go and make disciples of all nations, baptizing them in the name of the Father and of the Son and of the Holy Spirit, [20]and teaching them to obey everything I have commanded you. And surely I am with you always, to the very end of the age. (Matthew 28:18-20)

pALS Application

Perhaps ALS serves as a good reminder of how much we need God. Each loss of function makes us think more and more about how we must rely on God for every activity that makes us "alive." Of all the losses of function, loss of breath is the last in this life. Scriptures often speak of the deaths of the patriarchs as he breathed his last. (Genesis 25:8; 35:29; 49:33)

But as we learn to trust more in God, the more we pray in faith. Consider Louie Giglio's quote at the beginning of this chapter: "Through Christ you can breathe again, inhaling the words of God that always surround you, exhaling word and deeds of praise that reflect all of who He is." Physical inhaling and exhaling both have their counterparts in the spiritual realm.

As Jonathan Edwards wrote, "Prayer is as natural an expression of faith as breathing is of life."[16] As we are grateful for those 20,000 physical breaths per day, we can also be grateful for the constant spiritual breath of life that Jesus offers us. The more we pray, the more we become prepared to breathe in the eternal breath of heaven. It is there in heaven that we will have an even greater understanding of all the names of Jesus and our restoration in Him.

Closing Prayer

Heavenly Father, may we trust in Your Son, Jesus, and all that He has done for us. Jesus, we acknowledge that You have given us breath to fill our lungs and make us alive in this world. You have also given us the breath of Your Spirit to fill our hearts.

Help us, Lord, to exhale all our sin, then inhale Your forgiveness. Help us inhale the breath of life in the Word of God, in You Jesus and in Your Spirit. And then, with all our breath, may we exhale Your praises, Mighty God.

Let us do as Jude suggests:

> But you, dear friends, by building yourselves up in your most holy faith and praying in the Holy Spirit, [21]keep yourselves in God's love as you wait for the mercy of our Lord Jesus Christ to bring you to eternal life. (Jude 20-21)—Amen.

Reflections on Jesus as the Giver of the Breath of Life

1. Consider with thanksgiving that God has already breathed life into your lungs. Ask Him now to fill you with His Spirit.

2. After Jesus breathed on His disciples, so that they would receive the Spirit, He then spoke of forgiveness. Is there anyone you need to forgive now?

3. How can you let them know the way of forgiveness and salvation, too?

4. Practice exhaling your sins, and inhaling forgiveness; then practice inhaling the words of God, and exhaling words of praise.

8. Additional Scriptures for Meditation

*Throughout this Chapter, certain words have been rendered in **bold** type for emphasis. They do not appear that way in the original translation.*

Jesus, the Word—The Power of the Word of God

- Our gospel came to you not simply with **words** but also with **power**, with the Holy Spirit and deep conviction. (1 Thessalonians 1:5)

- Remember your **word** to your servant, for you have given me hope. (Psalm 119:49)

- All **Scripture** is God-breathed and is useful for teaching, rebuking, correcting and training in righteousness, [17]so that the servant of God may be thoroughly equipped for every good work. (2 Timothy 3:16-17)

- Do your best to present yourself to God as one approved, a worker who does not need to be ashamed and who correctly handles **the word of truth.** (2 Timothy 2:15)

- Let no corrupt **word** proceed out of your mouth, but what is good for necessary **edification**, that it may impart grace to the hearers. (Ephesians 4:29 NKJV)

- For our struggle is not against flesh and blood, but against the rulers, against the authorities, against the powers of this dark world and against the spiritual forces of evil in the heavenly realms...[17]Take the helmet of salvation and the sword of the Spirit, which is **the word of God.** (Ephesians 6:12,17)

- I am laid low in the dust; preserve my life according to **your word**. (Psalm 119:28)

- Turn my eyes away from worthless things; preserve my life according to **your word**. (Psalm 119:37)

- Remember **your word** to your servant, for you have given me hope. (Psalm 119:49)

Jesus, the Bread of Life—The Compassion of God

- All creatures look to you, to give them their food at the proper time. ²⁸When you give it to them, they gather it up; **when you open your hand, they are satisfied with good things.** (Psalm 104:27-28)

- I will praise you as long as I live, and in your name I will lift up my hands. ⁵I will be fully satisfied as with the **richest of foods**; with singing lips my mouth will praise you. (Psalm 63:4-5)

- Then the Lord said to Moses, "I will rain down **bread from heaven** for you. The people are to go out each day and gather enough for that day." (Exodus 16:4)

- Moses said, "This is what the Lord has commanded: 'Take an omer of manna and keep it for the generations to come, so they can see the **bread** I gave you to eat in the wilderness when I brought you out of Egypt." (Exodus 16:32)

- He humbled you, causing you to hunger and then feeding you with manna, which neither you nor your ancestors had known, to teach you that man does not live on **bread** alone but on **every word that comes from the mouth of the Lord.** (Deuteronomy 8:3)

- They asked, and he brought them quail; he fed them well with the **bread of heaven.** (Psalm 105:40)

- He has caused his wonders to be remembered; the Lord is gracious and compassionate. ⁵He provides **food** for those who fear him; he remembers his covenant forever. (Psalm 111:4-5)

- Then Jesus called His disciples unto Him and said, "I have compassion on the multitude, because they continue with Me now three days, and have nothing to **eat**: and I will not send them away fasting, lest they faint in the way." (Matthew 15:32)

- Therefore I tell you, do not worry about your life, what you will eat or drink; or about your body, what you will wear. Is not life more than **food**, and the body more than clothes? (Matthew 6:25)

- For the kingdom of God is not a matter of **eating and drinking**, but **of righteousness, peace and joy in the Holy Spirit.** (Romans 14:17)

- For I received from the Lord what I also passed on to you: The Lord Jesus, on the night he was betrayed, took **bread**, 24and when he had given thanks, he broke it and said, "This is my body, which is for you; do this in remembrance of me." 25In the same way, after supper he took the cup, saying, "This cup is the new covenant in my blood; do this, whenever you drink it, in remembrance of me." 26For whenever you eat this **bread** and drink this cup, you proclaim the Lord's death until he comes. (1 Corinthians 11:23-26)

- Jesus said to them, "Very truly I tell you, it is not Moses who has given you the bread from heaven, but it is my Father who gives you **the true bread from heaven.** 33For the bread of God is the bread that comes down from heaven and gives life to the world." 34"Sir," they said, "always give us this bread." 35Then Jesus declared, "**I am the bread of life.** Whoever comes to me will never go hungry, and whoever believes in me will never be thirsty. 36But as I told you, you have seen me and still you do not believe. 37All those the Father gives me will come to me, and whoever comes to me I will never drive away. 38For I have come down from heaven not to do my will but to do the will of him who sent

me. ³⁹And this is the will of him who sent me, that I shall lose none of all those he has given me, but raise them up at the last day. ⁴⁰For my Father's will is that everyone who looks to the Son and believes in him shall have eternal life, and I will raise them up at the last day."
(John 6:32-40)

Jesus, the Giver of Living Water—Our Source of Hope

- With joy you will draw water from **the wells of salvation.** (Isaiah 12:3)

- Whoever believes in me, as Scripture has said, **rivers of living water** will flow from within them. (John 7:38)

- You, God, are my God, earnestly I seek you;
  I thirst for you, my whole being longs for you,
  in a dry and parched land where there is no **water.**
  (Psalm 63:1)

- As **the deer pants for streams of water,**
    so **my soul pants for you, my God.**
  ²**My soul thirsts for God,** for the living God.
    When can I go and meet with God?
  ³**My tears have been my food** day and night,
  while people say to me all day long,
    "Where is your God?"
  ⁴These things I remember as I **pour out my soul:**
  how I used to go to the house of God
    under the protection of the Mighty One
  with shouts of joy and praise among the festive throng.
  ⁵Why, my soul, are you downcast?
    Why so disturbed within me?
  Put your **hope in God,**
  for I will yet praise him,
    my Savior and my God. (Psalm 42)

- The Lord answered Moses, "Go out in front of the people.
  Take with you some of the elders of Israel and take in your
  hand the staff with which you struck the Nile, and go. ⁶I will
  stand there before you by the rock at Horeb. Strike the rock,
  and **water** will come out of it for the people to drink." So

Moses did this in the sight of the elders of Israel.
(Exodus 17:5-6)

- He split the rocks in the wilderness
  and gave them **water** as abundant as the seas;
  ¹⁶he brought streams out of a rocky crag
  and made **water** flow down like rivers. (Psalm 78:15-16)

- Tremble, earth, at the presence of the Lord,
  at the presence of the God of Jacob,
  ⁸who turned the rock into a pool,
  the hard rock into **springs of water**. (Psalm 114:7-8)

- He turned the desert into **pools of water**
  and the parched ground into **flowing springs**;
  ³⁶there he brought the hungry to live,
  and they founded a city where they could settle.
  (Psalm 107:35-36)

- You care for the land and **water** it; you enrich it abundantly.
  The streams of God are filled with water
  to provide the people with grain,
  for so you have ordained it. (Psalm 65:9)

- My people have committed two sins:
  They have forsaken me, **the spring of living water**,
  and have dug their own cisterns,
  broken cisterns that cannot hold water. (Jeremiah 2:13)

- Lord, you are the hope of Israel;
  all who forsake you will be put to shame.
  Those who turn away from you will be written in the dust
  because they have forsaken the Lord,
  the spring of living water. (Jeremiah 17:13)

- But blessed is the one who trusts in the Lord,
  whose confidence is in him.
  ⁸They will be like a tree planted by the **water**

that sends out its roots by the **stream**.
It does not fear when heat comes;
 its leaves are always green.
It has no worries in a year of drought
 and never fails to bear fruit. (Jeremiah 17:7-8)

- Blessed is the one
 who does not walk in step with the wicked
or stand in the way that sinners take
 or sit in the company of mockers,
²but whose delight is in the law of the Lord,
 and who meditates on his law, day and night.
³That person is like a tree planted by **streams of water**,
 which yields its fruit in season
and whose leaf does not wither—
 whatever they do prospers. (Psalm 1:1-3)

- For I will **pour water** on the thirsty land,
 and **streams** on the dry ground;
I will **pour out my Spirit** on your offspring,
 and my blessing on your descendants. (Isaiah 44:3)

- But whoever drinks the water I give them will never thirst.
 Indeed, the water I give them will become in them a **spring of water** welling up to eternal life. (John 4:14)

- They shall neither hunger anymore nor thirst anymore; the
 sun shall not strike them, nor any heat; ¹⁷for the Lamb who
 is in the midst of the throne will shepherd them and lead
 them to **living fountains of waters**. And God will wipe away
 every tear from their eyes. (Revelation 7:16-17 NKJV)

- Then the angel showed me **the river of the water of life**, as
 clear as crystal, flowing from the throne of God and of the
 Lamb... (Revelation 22:1)

- The Spirit and the bride say, "Come!" And let the one who hears say, "Come!" Let the one who is thirsty come; and let the one who wishes take **the free gift of the water of life.** (Revelation 22:17)

Jesus, the Vine—Our Connections in God's Family

- I am **the true vine**, and **my Father is the gardener.** ²He cuts off every branch in me that bears no fruit, while every branch that does bear fruit he prunes so that it will be even more fruitful. ³You are already clean because of the word I have spoken to you. ⁴Remain in me, as I also remain in you. No branch can bear fruit by itself; it must remain in the vine. Neither can you bear fruit unless you remain in me. (John 15:1-4)

- **I am the vine; you are the branches.** If you remain in me and I in you, you will bear much fruit; apart from me you can do nothing. ⁶If you do not remain in me, you are like a branch that is thrown away and withers; such branches are picked up, thrown into the fire and burned. ⁷If you remain in me and my words remain in you, ask whatever you wish, and it will be done for you. ⁸This is to my Father's glory, that you bear much **fruit**, showing yourselves to be my disciples. (John 15:5-8)

- As the Father has loved me, so have I loved you. Now remain in my love. ¹⁰If you keep my commands, you will remain in my love, just as I have kept my Father's commands and remain in his love. ¹¹I have told you this so that my joy may be in you and that your joy may be complete. ¹²**My command is this: Love each other** as I have loved you. ¹³Greater love has no one than this: to lay down one's life for one's friends. ¹⁴You are my **friends** if you do what I command. ¹⁵I no longer call you servants, because a servant does not know his master's business. Instead, I have called you **friends**, for everything that I learned from my Father I have made known to you. ¹⁶You did not choose me, but I chose you and appointed you so that you might go and bear fruit—fruit that will last—and so that whatever you ask in my name the Father will give you. ¹⁷**This is my command: Love each other.** (John 15:9-17)

- And let us consider how we may **spur one another on toward love and good deeds**, ²⁵not giving up meeting together, as some are in the habit of doing, but **encouraging one another—** and all the more as you see the Day approaching. (Hebrews 10:24-25)

- So, my brothers and sisters, you also died to the law through the body of Christ, that you might **belong** to another, to him who was raised from the dead, in order that we might bear fruit for God. (Romans 7:4)

- Therefore we do not lose heart. Though outwardly we are wasting away, yet inwardly we are being renewed day by day. ¹⁷For our light and momentary troubles are achieving for us an eternal glory that far outweighs them all. ¹⁸So **we fix our eyes not on what is seen, but on what is unseen**, since what is seen is temporary, but **what is unseen is eternal.** (2 Corinthians 4:16-18)

Jesus, the Giver of Fruit—Our Growth in Christ

- Remain in me, as I also remain in you. No branch can bear **fruit** by itself; it must remain in the vine. Neither can you bear **fruit** unless you **remain in me.** (John 15:4)

- A shoot will come up from the stump of Jesse;
  from his roots a Branch will bear **fruit.**
  ²The Spirit of the Lord will rest on him—
  the Spirit of wisdom and of understanding,
  the Spirit of counsel and of might,
  the Spirit of the knowledge and fear of the Lord—
  ³and he will delight in the fear of the Lord. (Isaiah 11:1-3)

- Consider it pure joy, my brothers and sisters, whenever you face trials of many kinds, ³because you know that **the testing of your faith produces perseverance.** ⁴Let perseverance finish its work so that you may be mature and complete, not lacking anything. (James 1:2-4)

- Blessed is the one who does not walk in step with the wicked, or stand in the way that sinners take or sit in the company of mockers, ²but whose delight is in the law of the Lord, and who meditates on his law day and night.
  ³That person is like a tree planted by streams of water,
  which yields its **fruit** in season and whose leaf does not wither— whatever they do prospers. (Psalm 1:1-3)

- They will still bear **fruit in old age,** they will stay fresh and green, ¹⁵proclaiming, "The Lord is upright; he is my Rock, and there is no wickedness in him." (Psalm 92:14-15)

- But blessed is the one who trusts in the Lord, whose confidence is in him. ⁸They will be like a tree planted by the water that sends out its roots by the stream. It does not fear when heat comes; its leaves are always green. It has no worries in a year of drought and never fails to bear **fruit**. (Jeremiah 17:7-8)

- By their **fruit** you will recognize them. Do people pick grapes from thornbushes, or figs from thistles? [17]Likewise, every good tree bears **good fruit**, but a bad tree bears bad fruit. [18]A good tree cannot bear bad fruit, and a bad tree cannot bear good fruit. [19]Every tree that does not bear good fruit is cut down and thrown into the fire. [20]Thus, **by their fruit you will recognize them.** (Matthew 7:16-20)

- But the **fruit of the Spirit** is **love, joy, peace, forbearance, kindness, goodness, faithfulness,** [23]**gentleness and self-control.** (Galatians 5:22-23a)

- For this very reason, make every effort to **add to your faith goodness; and to goodness, knowledge;** [6]**and to knowledge, self-control; and to self-control, perseverance; and to perseverance, godliness;** [7]**and to godliness, mutual affection; and to mutual affection, love.** [8]For if you possess these qualities in increasing measure, they will keep you from being ineffective and unproductive in your knowledge of our Lord Jesus Christ. (2 Peter 1:5-8)

- Produce **fruit in keeping with repentance.** (Matthew 3:8)

- Do not get drunk on wine, which leads to debauchery. Instead, be filled with the Spirit, [19]speaking to one another with **psalms, hymns, and songs from the Spirit.** Sing and make **music from your heart to the Lord,** [20]**always giving thanks to God the Father for everything,** in the name of our Lord Jesus Christ. (Ephesians 5:18-20)

- May the God of hope fill you with all **joy and peace** as you trust in him, so that you may overflow with **hope** by the power of the Holy Spirit. (Romans 15:13)

- For this reason, since the day we heard about you, we have not stopped praying for you. We continually ask God to fill you with the knowledge of his will through all the wisdom and understanding that the Spirit gives, [10]so that you may live a life worthy of the Lord and please him in every way: bearing **fruit in every good work, growing in the knowledge of God.** (Colossians 1:9-10)

- And this is my prayer: that your love may abound more and more in knowledge and depth of insight, [10]so that you may be able to discern what is best and may be pure and blameless for the day of Christ, [11]filled with the **fruit of righteousness** that comes through Jesus Christ—to the glory and praise of God. (Philippians 1:9-11)

Jesus, our Good Shepherd—Our Rest in God

- Suppose one of you has a hundred sheep and loses one of them. Doesn't he leave the ninety-nine in the open country and go after the lost sheep until he finds it? 5And when he finds it, **he joyfully puts it on his shoulders** 6**and goes home.** (Luke 15:4-6a)

- The Lord is **my shepherd,** I lack nothing.
  2He makes me **lie down in green pastures,** he leads me beside quiet waters, 3he refreshes my soul.
  He guides me along the right paths for his name's sake.
  4Even though I walk through the darkest valley, I will fear no evil, for you are with me; your rod and your staff, they comfort me.
  5You prepare a table before me in the presence of my enemies. You anoint my head with oil; my cup overflows. 6Surely **your goodness and love will follow me** all the days of my life, and I will dwell in the house of the Lord forever. (Psalm 23)

- Come to me, all you who are weary and burdened, and I will give you **rest.** 29Take my yoke upon you and learn from me, for I am gentle and humble in heart, and you will find **rest for your souls.** 30For my yoke is easy and my burden is light. (Matthew 11:28-30)

- **My grace is sufficient for you,** for my power is made perfect in weakness. Therefore, I will boast all the more gladly about my weaknesses, so that Christ's power may rest on me. (2 Corinthians 12:9)

- But **he gives us more grace.** That is why Scripture says: "God opposes the proud, but shows favor to the humble." (James 4:6)

- Know that the Lord is God. It is he who made us, and we are his; we are **his people, the sheep of his pasture.** (Psalm 100:3)

- Surely **he took up our pain**
  and bore our suffering,
  yet we considered him punished by God,
  stricken by him, and afflicted.
  [5]But he was pierced for our transgressions,
  he was crushed for our iniquities;
  the punishment that brought us peace was on him,
  and by his wounds we are healed.
  [6]**We all, like sheep, have gone astray,**
  each of us has turned to our own way;
  and the Lord has laid on him
  the iniquity of us all. (Isaiah 53:4-6)

- The thief comes only to steal and kill and destroy; I have come **that they may have life**, and have it to the full. [11]I am the good shepherd. The **good shepherd lays down his life for the sheep.** (John 10:10-11)

Jesus, the Breath of Life—Our Eternal Life to Come

- **He himself gives everyone life and breath** and everything else...27God did this so that they would **seek him and perhaps reach out for him and find him**, though he is not far from any one of us. 28"For in him we live and move and have our being." (Acts 17:25b,27-28)

- For God so loved the world that he gave his one and only Son, that whoever believes in him shall not perish but have **eternal life**. (John 3:16)

- Jesus answered, "I am the way and the truth and the **life**. No one comes to the Father except through me." (John 14:6)

- Then the Lord God formed a man from the dust of the ground and breathed into his nostrils the **breath of life**, and the man became a living being. (Genesis 2:7)

- The Spirit of God has made me; the **breath of the Almighty** gives me life. (Job 33:4)

- As long as I have life within me, the **breath of God** in my nostrils, 4my lips will not say anything wicked, and my tongue will not utter lies. (Job 27:3-4)

- And you have praised the gods of silver and gold, bronze and iron, wood and stone, which do not see or hear or know; and the **God who holds your breath in His hand** and owns all your ways, you have not glorified. (Daniel 5:23b NKJV)

- All **Scripture is God-breathed** and is useful for teaching, rebuking, correcting and training in righteousness, 17so that the servant of God may be thoroughly equipped for every good work. (2 Timothy 3:16-17)

- Very truly I tell you, whoever **hears my word and believes** him who sent me has **eternal life** and will not be judged but has crossed over from death to **life**. (John 5:24)

- Now this is **eternal life**: that they know you, the only true God, and Jesus Christ, whom you have sent. (John 17:3)

- Let **everything that has breath** praise the Lord. Praise the Lord. (Psalm 150:6)

Restoration in the Book of Revelation

In heaven, we who believe in Jesus will be redeemed and restored. And the names of Jesus will be fulfilled and displayed. The book of Revelation reveals the truth of our eternal destiny.

The Word of God and our Words

Jesus who gave His life for us that we might live by faith in Him as our Messiah is described in Revelation:

> He is dressed in a robe dipped in blood, and his name is **the word of God**. (Revelation 19:13)

And our speech will be restored. We will be able to speak, even shout again in praise to God!

> Then I heard what sounded like a great multitude, like the roar of rushing waters and like loud peals of thunder, **shouting: "Hallelujah!** For our Lord God Almighty reigns." (Revelation 19:6)

The Bridegroom's Banquet and the Water of Life

We will be able to eat and drink again!

> Never again will they hunger; **never again will they thirst.** (Revelation 7:16)

And we will be invited to dinner with our Lord:

> Then the angel said to me, "Write this: Blessed are those who are invited to **the wedding supper of the Lamb!"**... [Jesus says]"To the thirsty I will give water without cost from the spring of **the water of life.**" (Revelation 19:9; 21:6)

Crowns for Fruitful Perseverance

It is there in heaven that we will receive crowns for the fruit of our labors.

> Blessed is the one who **perseveres under trial** because, having stood the test, that person will receive **the crown of life** that the Lord has promised to those who love him. (James 1:12)

Connections in Worship

And we may join the elders in the book of Revelation, casting our crowns before the throne of God:

> Whenever the living creatures give glory, honor and thanks to him who sits on the throne and who lives for ever and ever, 10the twenty-four elders fall down before him who sits on the throne and worship him who lives for ever and ever. They **lay their crowns before the throne** and say:
>
> 11"You are worthy, our Lord and God,
> to receive glory and honor and power,
> for you created all things,
> and by your will they were created
> and have their being." (Revelation 4:9-11)

Restoration by our Good Shepherd

> For the Lamb at the center of the throne will be their **shepherd**; 'he will lead them to **springs of living water**. And God will **wipe away every tear from their eyes.** (Revelation 7:17)

Reflections on Restoration in the Book of Revelation

1. The book of Revelation, although hard to understand, contains many precious promises. Which of the verses above make you most eager to experience heaven? Why?

2. Having considered all the names of Jesus in this devotional, which has brought you closest to Him?

   - Jesus, the Word
   - Jesus, the Bread of Life
   - Jesus, the Giver of Living Water
   - Jesus, the Vine
   - Jesus, the Giver of the Fruit of His Spirit
   - Jesus, the Good Shepherd
   - Jesus, the Giver of the Breath of Life

   Explain what that name means to you, and write it here (and on the next page, as needed) in a prayer of gratitude.

Epilogue

My wife was asked by several people, "Why not title your devotional "A Loving Savior?" As we discussed it, I told her I liked the title "A Living Savior." The fact that Jesus is a Living Savior means that He is in our real and relevant experience. He is not only a God of the past, or of the future. Our God has a presence that can be known today.

Knowing Jesus is our Living Savior draws the reader in. He is Life itself, the fullness of life—the life that everyone wants to have. He is the Way, the Truth, and the Life. When you draw near to Him, you experience His presence of joy, peace, and love.

A lot of Sharon's book includes stories about Jesus' life interacting with His disciples. He was the Son of God and Son of man, a living person available to them. When we come to Jesus, we find that He is always available to us, too. He is *still* **our very present help** in time of need. When we meet Him, we realize how much we are loved. We realize that He is our Living Savior and our Loving Savior as well.

Tom

God is our refuge and strength, A very present help in trouble. (Psalm 46:1 NKJV)

References

1. Charles H. Spurgeon. Charles Haddon Spurgeon Quotes (Author of Morning and Evening, Based on the English Standard Version) (goodreads.com)

2. Bart Millard and Pete Kipley, Lyrics Essential Music Publishing, Warner Chappell Music, Inc. Lyrics Licensed & Provided by LyricFind. Word of God Speak. 2002. MercyMe - Word of God Speak Lyrics | Lyrics.com

3. Jentezen Franklin. Jentezen Franklin (Author of Fasting) (goodreads.com)

4. Max Lucado. Top 25 Quotes by Max Lucado. | A-Z Quotes (azquotes.com)

5. Oswald Chambers. Top quotes by Oswald Chambers. quotemaster.org

6. Corrie ten Boom. Top quotes by Corrie Ten Boom. quotemaster.org

7. Oswald Chambers. Top quotes by Oswald Chambers. quotemaster.org

8. R.C. Sproul. R.C. Sproul Quotes (Author of The Holiness of God) (goodreads.com)

9. Hanibal Rodriguez. A Love that Finds Grace. Full Contemporary Service | Sermons | Wheaton Bible Church

10. R.C. Sproul. The Fruit of the Spirit by R. C. Sproul | Monergism

11. R.C. Sproul. 30 R.C. Sproul Quotes to Renew Your Mind (prayer-coach.com)

12. R.C. Sproul. R. C. Sproul quote: Prayer is to the Christian what breath is to life... (azquotes.com)

13. Louie Giglio. The Air I Breathe: Worship as a Way of Life. Multnomah Press, 2006. p. 120.

14. Steve White. Breathe. Thrive Global. | Medium

15. R.C. Sproul. Top 30 quotes of R. C. SPROUL famous quotes and sayings | inspringquotes.us (inspiringquotes.us)

16. Jonathan Edwards. Jonathan Edwards quote: Prayer is as natural an expression of faith as breathing... (azquotes.com)

Acknowledgements

First, I would like to acknowledge my husband of fifty years. Tom, you've had to walk with me through this awkward time. You've made every effort to surprise me by fulfilling my "bucket list" wishes (like visiting our favorite honeymoon sites again). And, even during this difficult year, you have re-created the happiest and most loving times of our 50 years together. Your faith is a constant reminder not to put my hope in this world, but in the next. I love you so much, Tom! AAMAJ!

I want to thank our daughters, Christy and Joy, who have been a constant source of rejoicing in my life:

Christy, your name has always demonstrated that you truly have the heart of a Christian daughter, wife, and mother of four, plus two new daughters-in-law. Your patience, wisdom and selfless love show through all you do. Being with you helps me rest in your kindness and in God's love. I love you so much, Christy! AAMAJ!

Joy, you have always lived up to your name, being cheerful and lighthearted, no matter your circumstances. Being a calm mother of five little ones exhibits your patience and selfless endurance. Your down-to-earth strength and reliance on God bring me a confident hope when I'm in your presence. I love you so much, Joy! AAMAJ!

Christy's husband, Mike, has been like my first son. I love both your fun-loving side, Mike, and your passionately caring nature. You are such a talented man, and a good provider for all in your care. You have always "been there" for me and Tom with love and concern and unwavering commitment to the best for us. I love you so much, Mike! AAMAJ!

Joy's husband, Aaron, you completed my hopes for two daughters and two sons. You are often "behind the scene" or "behind the camera," yet your sensitive love shows through all you do. Your creativity and fun-loving guidance for the children is over the top! As a passionate "PK" you observe all and respond to all, including Tom and me, with the thoughtful lovingkindness that comes from God. I love you so much, Aaron! AAMAJ!

And, Mike and Aaron, you have helped bring nine grandchildren into our lives as constant sources of happiness and affection. I so love you all—Joshua, Nathan, Andrew, Julia, Callie, Avery, Archer, Ryder, and Maverick! AAMAJ!

Joshua, you are an inspiration to me. You have always been an outstanding student, a Blackstone Fellow, a clerk to a federal judge, and now a lawyer. (You're the only Dille I never had in a homeschool class, yet you so kindly said that you learned a lot from my presence in your life.) And now that you have become an associate at a law firm, I am so eager to see how God will use you! Your words when you got cancer ("I had plans for my life, but God had a better one!") have been a motivation to me to trust God in my own illness. Now I long to see how all those plans will unfold in your life. I love you so much, Josh! AAMAJ!

Nathan, from the time you were little, you have been a tender-hearted, loving grandson. You paid close attention to all that people around you said and did, learning and growing from everything you observed. Now that you are a physics teacher, we know that your students must look up to you and admire you as much as we do. You never miss a chance to be helpful and encouraging, passing your faith along to youth at school and church. I love you so much, Nathan! AAMAJ!

Andrew, our third grandson, you are so uniquely individual. You have been an introspective, deeply caring, thoughtful and godly young man from an early age. You have been so articulate in speech and writing, so devoted and goal-oriented (even in the games we love to play with you!). Personally, I so treasure your willingness to learn my songs on the keyboard. I remember your compassion for me as you sang the verse about "my voice to You" from my song "My Life to You." I love you so much, Andrew! AAMAJ!

Julia, our first granddaughter, you have always shined like a jewel ever since you were born. You bring a happy outlook to every occasion, as I remember you singing "The Sun will Come out Tomorrow" on stage when you were only about six. You are an artist in so many ways, creating beauty on stage, on paper, in arts-n-crafts and cooking, and in all your relationships. As you demonstrated in your recent baptism, I'm sure your life will continue to unfold revealing God's beauty in your life. I love you so much, Julia! AAMAJ!

Callie, Joy's first daughter, you started a whole new "joyful family." From your first years, I could see you were a thought-filled, observant young lady with a determined spirit. I love your passion for all the activities in which you've been involved, and also your sense of humor that engages people around you. From sports to artistry, to organizing activities for your family, your kindness and good example will always be treasured. Your faith, demonstrated also in your recent baptism, will continue to shine to your siblings and friends. I love you so much, Callie! AAMAJ!

Avery, you are a delightful little girl always making me smile with your playful antics. Your bright and funny conversations catch me off-guard as I wonder what you will think of next. You love to take pictures because, as you said, it helps you remember "all the beautiful things." Your joy of living inspires me to have gratitude for every day. I love you so much, Avery! AAMAJ!

Archer, you are the most outgoing child I have ever known! You never hide what you are feeling, thereby encouraging others to do the same. I'll never forget the day I was swirling around in the hot tub with you as a three-year old. You said it reminded you of a couple getting married. You said, "We could get married, Grandma. I'm a boy and you're a girl, and I love you." "Are you asking me to marry you?" I replied. "No, Grandma, just pretending, but I do love you!" I do love you so much too, Archer! AAMAJ!

Ryder, I'm so sorry that we haven't been able to have conversations. Just as I was losing my voice, you started speaking. You call me by name, "Gamma" though you are still puzzled by my speech app. But now that you are two, you are growing in patience and understanding. You take my hand to come and do puzzles together, or dig in the sand with me. You bless me with your peaceful personality, full of love. And I love you so much, Ryder! AAMAJ!

Maverick, baby Mav, you are already so watchful of each one as we hold you. I cannot wait to see how your handsome little face will develop as your personality grows. Will you demonstrate your name as a bright star or an independent thinker as you grow up? Our world needs both, a light to shine for God's glory and a bold leader in our troubled world. I already love you so much, Mav! AAMAJ!

And now...Special thanks to our married grandsons and their wives, for we now have 11 grandchildren. Joshua when you married Allie, you chose such a kind and helpful, always encouraging, always affectionate, godly woman. Allie, you will make such a perfect counselor, as you are such a wonderful listener filled with concern for others. I love you so much, Allie! AAMAJ!

And Nathan, when you chose Colleen to marry, you found such a warm, effervescent, caring and compassionate woman of bold faith, always reassuring and cheering people on. Colleen, I know you will bless others by providing them with recreational therapy as much as you have already been a blessing to me. I love you so much, Colleen! AAMAJ!

And now thanks to those of our spiritual family as well. With much gratitude to our friends from Wheaton Bible Church and its small groups, inspiring pastors, teachers, and staff. Thank you to the people of Koinonia, and to our inspiring leaders and teacher, led by Greg and Beth Froese, and to our inspiring teacher, Dr. Andrew Schmutzer. You all have been unending in your kind encouragement of Tom and me.

I so appreciate our women's Bible study group, called "A Place For You." I joined this group ten years ago, and now it feels not only like "a place," but feels like home. Our small group truly fulfills the nickname we gave ourselves, the "Burden Babes" (based on Galatians 6:2). Thank you for being unafraid to help carry whatever loads we bring to the group. I have a special heart of thanks to Leslie Chall and to Laura Atkinson, for leading our small group and blessing me with your love and prayers.

None of this would have been possible without our overwhelmingly kind women's ministry leaders. Kellie

Kammes, Donna Stone, and Christine Walraven, and all dear coaches on our Core Team, your hard work for the Kingdom—with wisdom, care, humility, and perseverance—has brought great fruit. You give so unselfishly of your time, and you have reached out to me with such love!

I am so grateful for friends who emerged from online groups to reach out to me. Ann Chastain, Co-founder of the "Blessing Love Box" group has been an awesome support. Thank you—not only for assembling the original box of medical supplies for tube-fed patients like me—but your frequent checking-in has blessed me with a new friendship (even though we've never met.)

Ann introduced me to Chuck Graham, a retired attorney, author, and founder of *Ciloa* (Christ Is Lord Of All). The Ciloa ministry focuses on sharing God's love by encouraging others and teaching them how to become encouragers. Chuck's motivation grew out of his own experiences supporting his father with ALS. If possible, I would give an enormous "round of applause" to Chuck, for the great amount of time he spent editing and refining my grammar, expression, and Scriptural quotes. His help has been invaluable. Chuck, I appreciate your help and your fellowship so much.

Special gratitude to the ALS Family of Faith, and its founder, Steve Cochlan. Despite your own experience of ALS, you kindly took time to go through my manuscript and offer suggestions. We share a common goal of bringing hope and faith to other pALS.

Special thanks to pastors and friends from our daughters' churches: Living Hope Church, including our co-grandparents, Pastor Mike Gates and his wife Gayla; and,

Village Church of Bartlett, including Pastor Mike Boyle and his wife Meloday. I so appreciate all of you for your kind outreaches of hope.

Much appreciation to my doctors and nurses, dieticians and various therapists who have strived to make life as comfortable as possible for me.

I cannot name enough of you who have shown such lovingkindness to me. I love you all!

Made in the USA
Columbia, SC
09 September 2022

66865321R00061